HILL ECONOMY

HILL ECONOMY

R. JEYAKUMAR

SERIALS PUBLICATIONS
NEW DELHI

First Published - 2006

ISBN: 81-8387-055-4

Published by

SERIALS PUBLICATIONS
4830/24, Prahlad Street, Ansari Road
Darya Ganj, New Delhi-110002 (India)
Phone : 23245225. Fax : 91-11-23272135
E-mail: serials@satyam.net.in

DEDICATED
TO
THE MEMORY OF
My beloved father
who taught me the Values
of Education through
hard work

CONTENTS

PREFACE

"The Horse is made ready for the day of battle
but victory comes from the Lord". The Bible.

This book is based on the Ph.D. thesis of the author, that looks into the hill economy, particularly the socio-economic conditions of the inhabitants of Palamathi hills in Vellore District of Tamil Nadu state. The main occupation of these people are agriculture though the mountain dwellers look like people in the plains because most of them are migrants from the villages of vicinity. But their problems and challenges are entirely different from those faced in the plains. These peoples are not treated as "tribal" as many of them live below the required mountain height. Thus they forfeit the privileges accorded to the tribal population.

Most of the problems faced by them include basic amenities such as absence of hospital, lack of transport, nonavailability of proper shops etc. The inhabitant's demand for employment in the hill that can be met by developing factories or industrial establishments. The promotion of tourism industry which has plenty of scope to provide job opportunities can also be planned. By implementing the minimum wages Act for agricultural labours, improvement of hill farm through irrigation facilities, recognition of hill as special and distinct from lowland would facilitate resource flows to and from the hill. This will lead to increased income to hill communities and fair distribution of earnings from natural resources and services that will enhance the hill economy of this region.

The general view of mountain areas, geographical area of forests, rural economy, socio-economic development are focused with detailed introduction and scope of the study. The second chapter deals with the important concepts and review of past studies. The various aspect of the study area is analyzed and presented in the third chapter. The approach adopted for the study is vividly described in the fourth chapter. The results discussed different parts like migration trend, socio-economic conditions of the inhabitants, poverty and development programs that are given in the fifth chapter. The summary, conclusion and policy implications form part of the last chapter.

It is hoped that this empirical study will be useful to policy–makers, sociologists, anthropologists, agricultural soil scientist, environmentalists, economist, administrators, academicians and social scientists. This study can also help in the aesthetic enhancement of this place that would lead to a revenue generating industry namely tourism, tourism policy makers would have in depth knowledge to draw the course of action to achieve tourism development. The study should also help to frame a proper perspective planning for developing the hill economy of this village and community in particular.

R. JEYAKUMAR

ACKNOWLEDGEMENTS

I submit all praise, glory and honour to the Almighty ,in making my research project a reality.

I extend my sincere and heartful thanks to my guide and supervisor, Dr. K. Padmanabhan, M.A., BL., Phd, Reader, Head of the Research Department of Economics, Sacred Heart college (Autonomous), Tirupattur, for his invaluable, meticulous and dedicated supervision. I cannot adequately express in words, my great sense of gratitude, as he has been the key factor for the continuation and completion of the research work. I have gathered many valuable ideas from him. I once again express my indebtedness and reverence to him from the bottom of my heart.

My special thanks are due to the former principal, Rev. Dr. P. Soundararaju, SDB of Sacred Heart College, Tirupattur, who had permitted me to do research work within the college campus. I am greatly indebted to Rev Dr. Thanislas, SDB, former principal, Sacred Heart College, Tirupattur, for his valuable suggestions and blessings. I sincerely thank the Management of Sacred Heart College, Rector, Rev. Dr. Maria Arokiam Kanaga, SDB, the principal, Rev. Dr. C.M. Varghese, SDB and vice-principal Rev. Fr. C. Anthony Raj, SDB, for their blessings and encouragement.

I wish to record my deep debt of gratitude to the members of the Doctoral Committee for their valuable suggestions and critical comments for improving the merit of the research.

I am profoundly thankful to Dr. T. Lakshmanaswamy, Reader in Econometrics, University of Madras, Mr. S. Sagaya Doss, M.A., M. Phil Lecturer in Economics, Sacred Heart College, Tirupattur, and Mr. Jothi Nehru, M.A., M. Phil, for their helpful support for the statistical data analysis in SPSS done in this study.

I sincerely thank the Director of Institute for Social Sciences & Research, Vellore for granting me leave and permission to accomplish my Ph.D. I also record gratefully his initiation and support during this period.

I thank the Librarians of Institute for Social Sciences & research Vellore, Sacred Heart College, Tirupattur, University of Madras, CDS, Tiruvananthapuram, MIDS, Chennai, Madurai Kamaraj University, for their help and co-operation in collecting literature pertaining to my research study.

I owe my gratitude to the panchyat president, Thiru N.K. Ragavan and the Assistant Village Officer, Thiru Arul by whom I gather relevant data for the present study. It is my privilege and pleasure to make special mention of Mr. Kamaraj, Geologist, PWD, Vellore, who gave me valuable suggestions and resource materials.

The inspiration for this study has come from the inhabitants of the Palamathi hill, for whom the researcher has worked for more than two years. The willing and spontaneous cooperation extended by them to the researcher in the data collection is acknowledged with thanks. If the study brings any benefit to the people of this hill, it would be a great reward for this work.

The unstinting prayer, support, help and source of inspiration that I received from my wife, Dr. Hilda Vasanthakaalam, Sr. Lecturer, KIST, Rwanda have far exceeded the limit of my expectations.

The progressive printers & the typist Mr. S. Thomas who helped me in the typing with patience and I wish to place on appreciation of his record of the neat and timely typing work. I also extend my sincere thanks to my friends Mr. S, Saravanan and Mr.Anil Kumar for their assistance in Computer Works.

On a personal note I wish to thank my family members for the encouragement of this research work particularly my parents and my wife.

1

INTRODUCTION

Mountain areas cover a significant part of the world's surface. About 10 per cent of the world's population lives in the mountains, while 40 per cent occupy the water-shed areas below them. Thus half of the world's population depends directly or indirectly on mountains. Mountains produce water, energy, mineral, forest and agricultural products and are areas of recreation. They also store the biological diversity necessary for the sustainability of human life[1].

The key for the uplift of rural economy in India lies in the development of agriculture. Because 80 per cent of the geographical area of the country is occupied by it and also nearly 80 per cent of population is depending directly or indirectly on agriculture. Forestry, which is bracketed with agriculture, has a lot of potentialities for improvement in the rural economy by providing innumerable goods and services and also the much-needed employment. But forest occupies 22.7 per cent of the total geographical area of India[2]. The total area of forest in Vellore district is 1612.29 sq km. The total forest in Palamathi Hill is 405.10 hectare[3].

The diversity in climate and vegetation of mountains as distinct from the homogeneity of the surrounding countryside also makes them attractive and recreational areas for the nearby population. The use of mountains is often highly seasonal. Thus they have little permanent population. Activities that may operate on a year-round basis, such as mining and Forestry, which employ a few people, are short-lived and consequently lead to few permanent settlements. Probably no other physical feature of the earth has so many assets and generates so little permanent settlement[4].

Development is a process of change in the present economic structure towards improvement. It is a function of conversion of the present situation towards betterment. It refers to economic growth, economic welfare, economic progress and secular change[5].

In any developing country, there is a growing concern on the social and economic condition especially in the rural areas. They have an influence on the standard of living and the quality of life of the people.

Agriculture forms the backbone of rural economy, and it is the basis for existence in rural areas. However, agricultural progress is normally regarded as a pre-requisite of economic development and is associated with industrialization. It can follow only on the sound heels of agriculture[6].

Rural development is defined as improving living standards of the mass of the low-income population residing in rural areas. Rural development does not take place due to crop production only but it also embraces a large complex of allied activities, such as improvement of livestock, fisheries, poultry farming etc. Their comprehensive rural activities aim at socio-economic upliftment of the rural masses. They form a source of supplementary income during off-season to the farmers and the landless labours[7].

The inhabitants of a village may be farmers or traders or artisans or priests; and a village can be classified according to the occupation of the majority of its inhabitants. Villages may, moreover, belong to a single tribe, or may differ from one another in caste or religious persuasion, and this may give us another means of classification of types. But, the physical form taken by a village furnishes one of the most useful and objective means[8].

Moreover, their activities do not require much training and skill. Households and individuals are considered poor when the resources they command are insufficient to enable them to consume sufficient goods and services to achieve a reasonable minimum level of living. Households seek to mobilize them into a livelihood strategy, which is a mix of labour market involvement, savings, borrowing and investments, productive and reproductive activities, income labour and asset pooling and social networking. According to 1991 Census, agricultural labours constitute 40.1 per cent of the annual population[9].

The four components of socio-economic development viz., agricultural, industrial, social infrastructural and demographic are highly interlinked with one another. It means that the development of one component provided lever for the development of other components. Among these components agricultural development had highest link with social infrastructure development[10].

STATEMENT OF THE PROBLEM

The problems and constraints before mountain areas are complex requiring multi-dimensional interventions. Soil erosion, land slides, loss of biodiversity, and degradation of land and water resources are common problems throughout the region. The loss of these resources has had a cascading effect on mountain households both directly and indirectly.

The education and health delivery systems are very poor, particularly for women and children. Further more, the mechanism to impart the basic skills, needed for modern development activities, are lacking. Urgent changes are necessary to equip the population with the required skills for a better future. Development policies and programmes are not fully successful in this area. Today, international markets determine how local resources are to be used in many mountain areas. With non–availability of small-scale and agro based industries, institutions and weak inadequate human resource development, the process of development will be very slow.

The socio-economic condition of a place depends on the composition of the population, and caste, family size, dependency, age and sex-ratio, marital-status, level of education etc. Economic activities form the basis of household development. To this may be added migration, movements, maintenance of ties with rural areas, urban food production, and decisions about access to services such as education and housing, and participation in social net works.

Agriculture is the largest sector of the economic activity and it has a crucial role to play in the country's economic development by providing food and raw materials, employment to a very large proportion of population, capital for its own development and surpluses for national economy. In developing countries, the economic status of the people is directly related to production obtained from land and livestock.

The Vellore district has eight taluks. The Palamathi hill is a small range of hills that forms part of Vellore taluk. It depends entirely on agriculture and allied activities. The inhabitants of Palamathi hill village are wholly dependent on agriculture. But agriculture does not give good returns as they are using age-old agricultural practices and implements.

Agriculture provides seasonal employment and industrialization is absent. Shift in occupation is minimum and so unemployment prevails in this area to a very great extent. Lack of adequate connectivity in the village has delayed the development and growth of this place . Water shortage has hampered the agricultural front of Palamathi hills affecting irrigation, production and yield of crops. The geographical elevation of the place is obscure leading to soil-erosion and loss of soil fertility.

The people who inhabited the Palamathi hill village were the migrants from the surrounding places located in Tamil Nadu, Karnataka and Andhra Pradesh. What is their present socio-economic condition? Though they are living in the hills, they are not treated as tribals. So the special privileges enjoyed by the tribes are denied to them. The facilities available in the village are far from adequate compared to the plain. Then, why these people continue to stay in the hill? What are the development programmes implemented in the village? How far the people have derived benefit from these programmes? The present study is directed towards the above issues.

OBJECTIVES

1. To trace the origin and settlement details of the inhabitants of the Palamathi hills.
2. To examine the socio-economic conditions of the inhabitants of Palamathi hills.
3. To analyze the level of poverty prevailing among the people of Palamathi hills.
4. To identify and describe the role played by the development programs undertaken in the Palamathi hills.

HYPOTHESIS

1. The migrants of Palamathi Hills have travelled from far and near to the hill.
2. The development programmes have been benefited by more of the least income group than the higher income group.
3. There has been a slow change in the occupation of the inhabitants of Palamathi hill.

SCOPE OF THE STUDY

The Palamathi village is located at an elevation of 567.9 metre from the sea level. Most of the people living in the hamlets are migrants from in and around Vellore taluk. They came to this village in search of agricultural land for cultivation, fodder and the grass for cattle. However, today, the hamlet is fully denuded and the green cover has been completely exhausted. As a result, the people in the village find no scope for agriculture and no avenue for alternative employment. They face great hardships for survival. The present study is aimed at exploring the problems of the inhabitants of this village in terms of basic amenities, employment opportunities and scope for sustainable living.

The study will be useful to policy-makers, sociologists, anthropologists, agricultural soil scientists, environmentalists, economist, administrators, academicians and social scientists. It will help them to frame a proper perspective planning for developing the village. This study can also help in the aesthetic enhancement of this place that would lead to a revenue generating industry, namely tourism. Many schemes and projects have lead to the infrastructure development and maintenance of this hill village. Through this study, tourism policy makers would have in depth knowledge to draw the course of action to achieve tourism development. This can positively influence the socio-cultural and economic conditions of the inhabitants.

This study will enable the people of Palamathi to device a suitable strategy for their livelihood. This will lead to their economic upliftment and removal of poverty. Nearly half of the households, according to official records, are below the poverty line. In order to eliminate poverty, programmes aimed at generating adequate employment and income, wili have to the implemented. Finally, Palamathi is not recorded as hill station by the government. The present study will provide adequate information about the hill and it would emphasize the need for declaring this village as a hill station.

LIMITATIONS

Though the present study tries to find out the problems of the inhabitants of the Palamathi hills, it is not free from limitations. First, the present study relates to the hamlets inhabited by 1886 people living in 401 households. Thus, it is a location specific and micro level study. Therefore, the conclusions drawn can be applied only in similar areas elsewhere.

Second, the respondents have furnished their details from their memory. But, the researcher's long stay in the village and his participation in the village activities for more than two years minimizes this limitation.

Third, in this region, secondary data are not properly maintained. The researcher obtained such information from the Panchayat president that was retrieved from his memory and he had held this office portfolio continuously for 40 years.

Fourth, there is no separate meteorological station for this hill village and therefore the temperature and rainfall details of Vellore were used. The people and scientific experts believe that they are same in both the places.

Finally, the statistical errors crept in the calculations are minimized to the maximum extent possible.

PLAN OF THE BOOK

Chapter-I–Introduction, statement of the problem, objectives, hypotheses, scope, and limitations of the study are stated.

Chapter-II–Previous work and concepts relevant to the study are reviewed to define concepts and scope of the present study.

Chapter-III–A brief description of the study area is presented.

Chapter-IV–Design of the study, model formulation, and conceptual definition of specific variables are outlined.

Chapter-V–Results of analysis are presented and discussed with reference to the specific objectives to draw useful inferences.

Chapter-VI–Summary of findings, conclusions and implications of the results for policy and research are presented.

Annexure and bibliography are given at the end.

NOTES

1. Carr-Harris J. (Ed.) (1995), "Mountains and people-A Peoples Perspective from the Indian Himalayas".Sri Bhuvaneswari Mahila Ashram, Paper presented at the NGO Consultation Sustainable Development, Lima, Peru, p. 6.
2. Puspa Indurkar (1992), Forestry," Environment and Economic Development". Ashish Publishing House New, Delhi, p. 3.
3. District Census Book, 1991.
4. Ronald R. Boyce (1974), "The Basis of Economic Geography". Holt, Rinchart &Winston Publishers, New York City, U.S.A., pp. 57,59.
5. Puspa Indurkar, op. cit, p. 1.
6 Umalei: "Design of Rural Development, Lessons from Africa". Baltimore, John Hopkins Press 1975, p. 20.
7. Carold Rakodi (2002), A livelihood Approach Conceptual Issues and Definition in the Book Urban Livelihoods-A People Centered Approach to Reducing Poverty, Carold Rakodi and Tony Lioyd-Jones U.S.A., p. 328.

8. Desai A.R. (1969), "Rural Sociology in India". Popular Prakasam, Bombay, p. 206.
9. Statistical Outline of India (2000-2001), Tata Services Ltd., Department of Economics and Statistics. Bombay house Mumbai-400001, p. 32.
10. Dubey (1992), 'Process of Socio-economic Development', Rawat Publications, Jaipur p. 155.

2

REVIEW OF CONCEPTS AND LITERATURE

A review of concepts and previous studies is useful to define precisely the concepts used in the present study, to place the problem in proper perspective and to decide the frame work for analysis. Precise definition of the concepts would enable both the collection of relevant data, and meaningful interpretation of the results of analysis.

CONCEPTS

The important concepts reviewed in this chapter are: settlement, migration, hill economics, socio-economic condition, assets, cropping pattern, marketable surplus, poverty, employment, development, hill development, forest and tourism development.

Settlement

In English law a settlement denotes an instrument designed to regulate during a specific period, the enjoyment of property and to provide during the same period for the safe custody and prudent management of the subject matters of that property.[1]

The term "settlement" has got more than one meaning but in the settlement Geography, it is generally understood as a house or cluster of houses, including the surrounding land, usually grouped at a convenient site and generally without any formal plan, and it is a comparatively small and simple agglomeration of buildings.[2]

Types of Settlements

Settlements have evolved into two types: rural and urban-distinguished by the predominant type of economic activity undertaken by the residents.

Rural Settlement

Rural settlement, which have agriculture as a predominant occupation, differs from urban settlements.

Urban Settlement

Urban settlement, the principal occupation of the residents is secondary or tertiary.

Clustered Settlement

As people switched from hunting and gathering to settled agriculture, they apparently concentrated into settlement.

Clustered Rural Settlement

Clustered rural settlement, based on farming comprises of houses, farm structure, and other frequently used buildings, such as religious centers, with fields for grazing animals and growing crops surrounding the village building. The fields must be accessible to the farmer and are thus generally located within a radius at one or two miles from the village structures.

Dispersed Settlement

In the past two hundred years, dispersed settlement pattern, with most farmers living on isolated farms rather than villages, are becoming more common.[3]

Migration

According to the Economic Dictionary (John Black, 1997) migration means the movement of people between regions of countries. Immigration and emigration are usually reserved for migration into and out of countries.

Migration may be temporary with the intention of returning in the future to the permanent residents. Migration is affected by push and pull factors. Push factors include lack of employment opportunities, lack of other facilities and fears of disorder or of persecution on grounds of race, religion or politics in the areas people live. Pull factors include favorable employment opportunities, good health and educational facilities, public order and freedom favorable climate particularly for retirement, in the areas people move to.[4]

Kinds of Migration

Migration takes many forms and it can be classified in many ways. One basic division is between voluntary and involuntary migration, another is between short-term and long-term migration.[5]

Voluntry Migration

Migration is as old as human history. Voluntary migration means that the movement is to achieve a goal or protect an individual's interests, but population movement in modern times has wider social, ecological implications. Migration takes place in different forms in different areas, like rural-rural, rural-urban-rural and urban-urban.[6]

Internal Migration

When people of one country migrate from one place to other, without crossing the boundary of the status itself, it is called internal migration.

International Migration

When the people of one country leave their country of origin and migrate to another independent country that is known as international or out migration.[7]

Free Individual Migration

When we think of "immigration we usually think of the mass movement of Europeans to Australia, New Zealand, South Africa, and the Americans during the last two centuries.

This movement was unique in many ways. It involved greater ocean travel over open waters, greater numbers, long distance, and more voluntary, individual, and peaceful movement than had ever been known before. It was a phenomenon new to the world and one not likely to be seen again. Yet its very massiveness regency colours much of our thinking about human migration.[8]

Controlled Migration

Gradually this free individual migration of the last two centuries is giving way to another kind-controlled migration. The rise of nationalism, with increasing state regulations, has inevitably led to a great control of human movement across national boundaries. Each nation now wants to regulate the number and kind of persons leaving as well as the number and kind arriving.

Most other nations also now have strict legislation aimed at controlling the quantity and kind of immigrants, admitted . Even Latin America, which professes to need immigrants, generally excludes Asiatic and wants only Europeans of certain types.[9]

Motives for Migration

There are many factors that motivate migrants. At all times most important factor which motivated people to migrate was economics. The people migrated and continue to migrate either to have better living or to have a living for themselves and their families. In the present study the inhabitants are mainly migrating for employment and agriculture.[10]

Hill Economics

A hill is an elevation of land rising a few hundred feet above surrounding country. Some hills are formed by glaciers, which leave stone and sand when they melt, others are produced by the gradual wearing down of high lands. Hills are pleasant to see in any country that is generally at high level. When many hills are close together they may become famous for their scenic beauty. The Berkshire Hills in Massachusetts are covered with trees and grass as carpets, and are so beautiful, that many people admire them as much as the highest mountains. There is no precise difference between a hill and a mountain. Hills are generally smaller, although some mountains are called hills. For example, the highest point the Berkshires is 3,505 feet. Hill located near the base of a mountain range are called foot hills.[11]

Mountains

Mountains do not fit well into either a foreboding land concept or a good land concept. Certainly they are sparsely inhabited and in this regard might be considered as foreboding for settlements. In as much as there is an altitude counterpart in climate, vegetarian and soils that correspond to the latitude related patterns discussed above; mountains must, therefore, be considered a mixture of possibilities- some foreboding, others ideal.[12]

Socio Economic Condition

The socio-economic conditions of a place reveals the composition of the population, the social characteristics. viz., marital-status, level of education etc. and the economic status as type and status of activity, employment sector and the like. The socio-economic scenario varies from region to region and place to place, country to country. The socio-economic picture of one village is different from another village of the state. However, the employment opportunities, whether organized or unorganized would influence the income earnings. This has an impact on the status of living and the quality of life.[13]

Nuclear Family

Nuclear family is based upon the individuality of the married couples, who separate themselves from their ancestral residence, so that inter–dependence between the couple, their children and the parents and grand-parents become minimized. Such family, generally consists of husband, wife and their children. Such a family is an autonomous unit free from the control of elders. It manages its own affairs, husband and wife taking part in family matters, and rearing the children. The nuclear family "lives" only until one of the parents die.

Extended Family

When several nuclear families merge, there is an extended or joint family, consisting of husband and wife, their son, son's wife and son's children, nieces and nephews, brothers, their wives and·children, uncle, aunt and their children's etc. Hindu families are of this type. It is a collection of more than the primary family. The extended family is continuous i.e., members many come and go but the group continues.[14]

Education

Education is an important component of social development. Many educationists have defined education. Heinrich Pestalozyi has defined education in the following words. "Education is nothing more than the polishing of each single link in the great chain that binds humanity together and gives it unity." "Gandhiji meant by 'education' an all-round training out of the best in child and man's body, mind and spirit"[15].

Health

The Masby Medical Encyclopedia defines health as "a state of physical, mental and social well-being and the absence of disease of other abnormal condition".[16]

The WHO defines health as a state of complete physical, mental and social well being and not merely an absence of disease or infirmity.[17]

Health is a state in which all the body organs and systems are normal and are functioning normally.[18]

Nutrition

Nutrition may be defined as the science of food and its relationship to health. It is conceived primarily with the part played by nutrients in body growth, development and maintenance. Good nutrition mean "maintaining a nutritional status that enables us to grow well and enjoy good health".[19]

Assets

Assets are possessions of value, both real and financial. Real assets include land, building, or machinery owned. Financial assets include cash and securities, and credit extended to customers.[20]

Fixed Assets

Fixed assets are properties acquired for permanent use in the business. The business earns its revenue by making use of these fixed assets. Plant and machinery, land and buildings etc., are examples of fixed assets.[21]

Land

Generally by land we refer to the soil that is used or to be used for cultivation or for construction. But in economics land has a wider meaning. It includes not merely land in the ordinary sense of the term but the whole of the material and the forces which nature gives for man's aid in land and water. In air and light and heat. In other words, it comes, besides land, a great many things such as sun shine, rain, wind, water falls, seas, rivers, minerals, electricity, magnetism and animals, in a word, everything given free by nature and economically useful to man. Thus, the term, land, in economics denotes all natural resources available to man for producing wealth.[22]

Classification of Lands

Areas that are too dry for farming cover approximately 20 per cent of the earth's land surface.

Wet Lands

Lands that receive very high levels of precipitation may also be inhospitable for human occupation.

Cold Lands

Few human beings live in very cold climate. Land around the North and South Poles, is covered by ice caps and consequently cannot support vegetation.

High Lands

Relatively few people live at high elevations. The highest mountains in the world are sparsely settled, for example, approximately half of Switzerland's land area is more than 1000 meters above sea level. But only 5 per cent of the country's people live there.[23]

Land Relations

The nature of land relation determines the share of various socio-economic groups associated with agriculture in the total agricultural wealth. For instance, in the Zamindari area, the Zamindar receives, by far, the larger share of agricultural income than the cultivating tenant. The staggering disparity between the colossal income of the former and the meager income of the latter is basically due to the Zamindari type of land relations has its own logic and its own law of development. Hence, we find that the general tendency of the agrarian economic development in the Zamindari Zone is to accentuate the economic contrast. Land relations play a decisive role in determining the degree of homogeneity or heterogeneity of rural population. In Zamindari area, the rural society is mainly divided into such groups as Zamindars, noncultivating tenants and sub-tenants, and finally cultivating tenants. In the ryotwari area, there are generally peasant proportions of various grades and landless workers. In the case of large-scale capitalist agriculture, there exist such groups as agrarian capitalists, farm managers, technicians, wage labourers and others.

The nature of land relations, which determines the share of material wealth of various sections engaged in agriculture, thereby, also determines the respective specific weight of those sections in the social, political, and cultural life of the rural society.

The nature of land relations will also decide the degree of stability and social harmony in the agrarian area. Land relations, by basically determining the share of various agrarian social groups in the total agricultural wealth, therefore, also decide how much is scope each of the total life of a society.[24]

Cropping-Pattern

Cropping-pattern refers to the crop-wise distribution of the cultivated land area, the changes in this distribution over-time and the determinants of this distributopn.[25]

Consumption

Consumption means the act of using goods and service to satisfy current wants. While, theoretically precise, there have been practical problems in using consumption, the main problem arises in the treatment of consumer durables.[26]

Marketed Surplus

Marketed surplus, on the other hand, represents only that portion of the marketable surplus which is actually marketed and is placed at the disposal of the non-farm rural and urban population. In case of commercial agriculture, the farmer, as he is motivated by profit considerations, takes his whole produce to the market and purchases his requirements from the market. But in subsistence agriculture, the farmer generally produces for his own subsistence and it is only the reminder left meeting his own requirements, is taken to the market for sale "Marketed surplus, on the Other hand refers to the actual quantity which enters into the market and as such, it is objective.[27]

Marketable Surplus

Marketable surplus represents the theoretical surplus available for disposal with the producer left after his genuine requirements of family consumption, payment of wages in kind, feed, seed and wastage, have been met. The farmer's retention is a matter of subjective guess and the concept of "marketable surplus" is subjective. Marketable surplus will always be less than the actual production. But it can be higher or lower than the level of marketed surplus during a period depending on the extent of hoarding from the current production, on the extent of de-hoarding of the accumulated stock by the producers. This means the "theoretical surplus available for disposal with the producer, left after this genuine requirements of family consumption, payment of wages in kind, feed, seed and wastage have been met".[28]

Income

It is the flow of money or goods of an individual or groups of individuals of a firm over same period of time."[29]

Expenditure

Expenditure is spending by consumers, investors, or the Government. Consumer expenditure is restricted to purchasing real goods and services; acquiring assets or making transfers to others by individuals is not counted as expenditure. Government expenditure is treated differently.[30]

Savings

Keynes defines savings as the sum of differences between the money income of individuals and the money expenditure on current consumption.[31]

Investment

Investment means the creation of new capital assets like construction of new buildings, new factories and so on. It is an expenditure on capital goods that increases the wealth of the community. But it is not an expenditure on consumers goods nor it is a deposit in the Bank.[32]

Borrowing

Incurring debts to finance spending is known as borrowing. This is done by individuals, firms and Governments. Borrowing appears desirable when the benefits from using borrowed money are greater than the interest costs. This may be because of urgent need for individual's spending of sudden falls in income or favorable investment opportunities for firms.[33]

Poverty

Meaning of Poverty

The state of one who lacks as usual or socially acceptable amount of money or material possessions is poverty. Poverty is said to exist when people lack the means to satisfy their basic needs. In this context, the identification of poor people first requires a determination of what constitutes basic needs. They may be defined as narrowly as "those necessary for survival" or as broadly as these reflecting the prevailing standard of living in the community[34].

According to Paul Samuelson and William D. Nordhans (1995), the word, "poverty" means different things to different people. Clearly, poverty is a condition in which people have inadequate incomes, but it is hard to draw an exact line between the poor and the non-poor. Economists have, therefore devised certain techniques which provide the official definition of poverty.

As a starting point, economists defined poverty as a level of income that is necessary to maintain a subsistence level of consumption. To double check this calculation, economists have noted that poor families generally spend one-third of their income on food. Hence from calculations on the cost of subsistence food budget, economists can calculate a minimum food budget by a factor of 3. In addition, poverty is a relative term. The notion of a subsistence budget includes subjective questions of taste and social conventions. Housing, i.e., today considered substandard often includes household appliances and plumbing that were unavailable to the wealthiest citizens of earlier era.[35]

It may however, be generally characterized as a state of deprivation, dependence and degradation below physically and socio-culturally acceptable standards.[36]

Poverty is defined on the basis of individuals or societies. Brown Rowntree (1902) has defined families were "total earnings are insufficient to obtain the minimum necessaries for the maintenance of merely physical efficiency"[37]. According to him, the biological need is of primary concern. But Holes Bawn has argued that ,poverty is always defined according to the conventions of the society in which it occurs.

However, it is very common to define poverty as a uni-dimensional poverty. As Wilbur (1973) noted, for practical purposes, it is easy and convenient to use as indicator like income as a certain and to define poverty in terms specific threshold.[38]

Poverty is a situation in which a section of the community is unable to acquire or get even the basic necessities of life such as minimum of food, clothing and shelter. When a substantial section of society is said to be suffering from mass poverty.[39]

Poverty in India

Poverty in India is not entirely an economic phenomenon, but is associated with groups which suffer from many deprivations in the field of education, employment, social and infrastructure services like water supply, sanitation, roads, electricity, housing, etc. Thus the problems, arising from social phenomena, need to be examined in a wider perspective involving various disciplines of social sciences.[40]

Demographic Perspective in Poverty

Demographic perspective is fundamental in the study of poverty. At the general level, poverty is related to population growth, fertility, mortality, morbidity and migration. At the specific level it is necessary to understand the socio-economic and demographic characteristics of the poor in the different income and expenditure groups.

The level of living of households is associated with size, age, lifecycle, sex, dependency ratio, skills of persons in the working age group, earning capacity in different sections of the economy, and the human capital dimensions of education, job training, health, nutrition and housing.[41]

Poverty Line

"Poverty Line" indicates minimum level of consumption and those people failing to get it at least are said to be below the poverty line.[42]

Poverty line refers to the cut-off level of annual income of the households. The households having annual income lower than the cut-off level of income are said to be poor.[43]

Poverty Gap

The poverty gap is defined as the aggregate short fall in income of all the poor persons when taken for the poverty line. In other words, poverty gap is the short fall of each person's income from the poverty line.

The formula for poverty gap is:

$$G = \Sigma (Z - Yi)$$

$$i = 1$$

Where,

G = poverty gap

Z = the poverty line

Yi = the income/expenditure of the ith household below the poverty line.[44]

Employment

Demand for Labour

According to the classical theory, the equilibrium of aggregate real output and employment is determined by the aggregate production function and labour's demand and supply schedules. The demand schedule for labour is derived from the aggregate production function. The aggregate production function shows that with a given capital stock, natural resources and technology, additional labour employed yields diminishing additional output.[45]

Unemployment

Unemployment is undoubtedly the most important economic problem that confronts the Indian economy. Unemployment means a tragic waste of manpower and the deprivation of society of the goods and services which could be produced by providing productive employment to the unemployed. Unemployment is also responsible for the hardships and low standard of living to the unemployed. If unemployment persists for long period, it breeds frustration and anger against the society that fails to provide work to the unemployed.

Rural Unemployment

Rural unemployment in India is also attributed to the shortage of capital and it can be broadly categorized into two classes.

Open Unemployment

This type of unemployment is among the agricultural labours, rural artisans and educated persons. Because of seasonal character of agriculture, there is a peak demand for labour at the time of sowing, weeding and harvesting operations, where as, demand for labour becomes too thin during slack season. The period of seasonal employment varies from state to state depending upon irrigation, fertility of land, agricultural technology and cropping intensity.

Concealed Unemployment

It is also called disguised unemployment and it is not possible to identify the unemployed. According to the U.N. Committee of Experts, the disguised unemployment are those persons, who work on their account and who are so numerous relatively to resources with which they work, that, if, a number of them were withdrawn to work in other sectors of the economy, the total output of the sector from which they were withdrawn would not be diminished even though no significant reorganization would occur in this sector. In rural India this type of unemployment is found among small and marginal farmers. Their land holdings are too small and fragmented to provide them full employment throughout the year. Like agricultural labours, they have to borrow from non-institutional agencies at high rate of interest both for production and consumption purposes. Due to financial constraints, they have not been able to start subsidiary occupations to add to their family income. When the family members fail to get employment outside agriculture, they settle on land leading to tiny and scattered holdings. Thus unemployment, poverty and illiteracy add to the number of disguised unemployed year after year in rural India.[46]

Develop ment

Meaning

According to Charles P. Kindle Berger and Bruce Herrick, "economic development since the mid-twentieth century has come to imply consciously sought and directed social change of a type and scope never before attempted.[47]

It is also said that "a philosophical argument can be made that the objective of economic development does not lie with material improvements themselves but with the increased opportunity for choice among alternatives and control of individual destiny which accompany higher incomes".

According to Meier and Baldwin (1976), "economic development is a process whereby an economy's real income increases over a long period of time.[48]

Economic growth and development means sustained increases in output per head, for, it is only by this that a community's living standards can rise over a long period. It is not sufficient to look at output growth in absolute terms, for, this could be obtained by disproportionate use of factor inputs with diminishing returns prevailing such that output per head might actually fall.[49]

Agricultural Development

Agricultural development itself depends upon the development of industries. Manufactured agricultural inputs like fertilizers and farm machinery are provided by the industrial progress. Prof. Kindle Berger correctly emphasizes this point when he says, "in order to increase the efficiency on the farm one must start in the factory." The increase in the nation's stock of capital on account of industrialization also stimulates the growth in the agricultural sector.

Agricultural development is an aspiration as well as a challenge, particularly in a developing country. It is an aspiration, as it signifies a drive towards a desirable future. The general belief that the farmers and particularly the Indian farmers, are traditional, fatalistic and slow of change, becomes a challenge in the process of agricultural development.[50]

Rural Development

Recall the face of the poorest and most helpless man whom you have seen and ask yourself if the step you contemplate is going to be of any use to him. Will he be able to gain anything by it? Will it lead into Swaraj self-rule for the hungry and also for the spiritually starved members of our countrymen?

Rural development is a strategy designed to improve the economic and social life of a specific group of people–the rural poor. It involves extending the benefits of development to the poorest among those who seek a livelihood in rural areas.[51]

Components of Rural Development

The various components which could be identified can be enumerated as follows:

(a) Agriculture proper i.e. cultivation of various crops, including wet crops like paddy and sugarcane, dry crops like sorghum and other millets and wheat as well as commercial crops like cotton and oil seeds.

(b) Agro-service including supply of inputs, credit and storage as well as marketing facilities.

(c) Agro- industrialization is connected with agro processing and agro-inputs.

(d) Allied agricultural activities include horticulture, dairy farming, poultry farming, sericulture, etc.

(e) Economic overheads for agricultural development, namely, irrigation, rural electrification, rural communication etc.

(f) Social overheads for development of rural community such as educational institutions, hospitals etc.

(g) Agrarian relationship, which are being restructured through land reform measures.

(h) Rural and village industries include Khadi, Handicraft, etc.

(i) Distribution of consumer goods to rural people.

(j) Re-constitution of rural institutions like village panchayat, youth club Mahilamandals etc.[52]

Village Development

The key to Swaraj is not the cities but the villages. When I succeed in ridding the villages of their poverty, I have won Swaraj for you and for the whole of India.*Gandhiji stressed the great importance of the village in the Indian school system and in order to drive home this truth, he even went to the extent of declaring that, if the villages perish India will perish too.*[53]

Rural Reconstruction

The Marthandam Practical Training School in rural reconstruction was built on a foundation of summer schools, held annually since 1926. These summer schools gave intensive training from 25 to 75 students each year, mostly honorary rural workers, who do so much in their spare time to improve their villages and who wished to become more efficient in the comprehensive programs they were trying to promote. These schools were short; but it was surprising how much ground could be covered by an intensive program of teaching and study on a limited number of subjects with the day's work starting at 5.30 in the morning and lasting till 9.30 at night. The students worked harder than they ever could in a long course and encouraging things has been that they actually went out and put into practice what they learned during these weeks.

This school has been helping to benefit all members of rural families, male and female, young and old, of different castes and religions, in all phases of their life-physical, mental, spiritual, social and economic. There is not much use in training students in one or two lines of improvement when the villages have to be helped on all sides of his life. The self-help basis is probably the only worth-while basis for development in any part of India.[54]

Hill Development

Mountains have considerable impact on the economic development of a country. Mountains, as a rule, restrict settlement to a large extent. High rugged mountains impose tremendous impediments upon the movement of people, the spread of population and the building of roads and railways. Development of agriculture and manufacturing become difficult, because of certain clearly discernible obstacles. Yet, mountains offer great benefit in certain definite ways.[55]

Forests

Forests include all lands classed as forest under any legal enactment dealing with forests or administered as forests, whether state owned or private, and whether wooded or maintained as potential forest land. The area of crops raised in the forests and grazing lands of the area open for grazing within the forests should remain included under the forest area.

Social Forestry Schemes

The primary objective of social forestry is to generate, through voluntary action , wood fuel, fodder and food for sustenance, there by, contributing to an environment friendly habitat.[56]

Transport

Transportation means the conveyance of persons or goods from one place to another. The need for conveyance of goods arises from the fact that they are produced in one place and desired in another. The transportation of persons arises from the need of individuals to go from one place to another to satisfy some need, whether connected with business or related to social , cultural or recreational interest.[57]

Irrigation

It is defined as the artificial application of water to land. It plays an important role on the economic development of Tamilnadu. The Irrigation Commission of 1972 remarked that Tamil Nadu is the only state which has utilized nearly 98 per cent of the potential created for irrigation through major sources.[58]

Tourism Development

Tourism is increasingly recognized as one of the most important sectors of the global economy. In India, although we have not yet even begun to tap the potential, tourism already is the third largest foreign exchange earner. Each million rupees invested in tourism creates 47.5 new jobs. This compares favorably to even important traditional sectors like agriculture, where a similar investment yields only 44.7 new jobs. World wide, countries at all stages of development, are realizing that tourism is an important engine of growth for new millennium. Tourism sector can help us our natural and cultural environments, providing sustainable development at many levels.[59]

REVIEW OF PAST STUDIES

Rural Settlements

Nagabhushana Rao (1989) had undertaken a study on the planning units for rural development. He has adopted the method of delimiting the area as dependent settlement, central village and service centers at the third level.

All settlements were visited during the field survey and the data were collected with the help of a field questionnaire. It consisted of 52 indicators covering socio-economic, cultural and political aspects. Enquiries were made with the progressive assistants, Extension officers, Village Development officers, head of the Panchayat, Patwari, the school teacher and village officers.

In this study these properties were used as a measure of centrality of settlements in addition to their population size. The type and volume of functions can be measured in several ways. For example one can simply count the presence of various functions in a settlement without weighing of them. But it may not be a proper one. Therefore, a more refined method of "Scalogram Analysis" had been applied.

The smallest planning units consists of the central villages and its hinterland. Further, along with the hierarchy of settlements, the service center being more central in character had large hinterlands. The units consisting of central places and the hinterland at the three hierarchy levels were the basic planning units we had set out to discover. The administrative authorities as well as other government agencies, therefore ought to recognize the importance of the hierarchy of these centers and devise the necessary plans for realizing the objective of an integrated development of the rural areas. Furthermore it facilitates the balanced development of a taluk.

It was therefore, concluded that this approach would help to provide the required services for the people in the taluk in an orderly manner and also lubricate the balanced development of the taluk. In the above study properties were used as a measure of centrality of settlements.[60]

Socio-Economic Conditions of the Rural Poor

Udaya Bhaskara Reddy (1986) had made a study on the socio-economic conditions of rural poor in Semiliguda block in Orissa. There were 350 house holds in his sample frame which comprised of 117 tribal household families, 103 other communities households. The data was collected by survey method. The study reported that the average annual family income of the sample house holds was Rs. 3,680.68. In the case of tribal households it was Rs. 3,542.53 and Rs. 3,853.24 for SCs, while it was Rs. 3,666.88 for other caste communities. The dependency ratio was 2.40 and the average annual per capita income was Rs. 786.47, while for the tribals it was only Rs. 742.63. the study also reported that the people in the block appeared to be living on bare subsistence. In fact, it was not only true for the block but appears to be applicable for most of the rural of the country.

The expenditure pattern was heavily weighed in favour of food grains followed by clothing. There was little expenditure on the items like education, travelling, and medicine.

The study also found out that 90 per cent of households had a per capita expenditure below Rs.1,200 per year. the average value of assets was Rs.711.43. Out of this 57.5 per cent was kept in the form of ornaments. Finally the study had recommended the introduction of dairy, poultry, piggery and fishery etc., which have high income generating potential but require low capital within short generation period, and the need for effective implementation of these steps will go a long way in improving the socio-economic conditions of rural poor.[61]

Gujjars in Punjab

Balbir Kumar and Karam Singh (1991-92) had conducted a study on the socio-economic problems of tribal Gujjars in Punjab in the 1991-92. The specific objectives of the study were: (i) to study the extent and role of pull and push factors for their migration to the state (ii) to identify the socio-economic characteristics of the migrants, activities. (iii) to analyze the investment pattern and (iv) to study the cost and returns from their major activities.

The study was conducted on the basis of snow ball sampling method. There were 69 sample families taken from Ludhiana, Jalandar, Kapurthala, Hashiarpur, Fatehgarh, Sangrur and Rojar districts in Punjab. The 69 sample families, comprised 28 small, 27 medium and 14 large dairy households. The data were collected by interview method. Simple averages and percentages were used to analyse the data. The study also reported that the average family size of the Gujjars was 5.5, of which, 3.8 were earners indicating a dependency ratio of 1.4. They were also found to be illiterate. The study also reported that the average asset value of the tribal Gujjars was about Rs.90,000,and the asset values ranged between Rs.56,000 on small category to Rs. 173,000 on the large category households. The study also found that dairy was the major source of their livelihood . The average net cash income from dairy was Rs. 37,000 per annum. Finally, the study concluded that the households with medium and large herd size had good income levels and thus have started raising their living standards.[62]

Constraints of Tribal Economy

Oberol R.C. et. al. (1986-87), had made a study on the socio-economic status and constraints of tribal economy, Kinnavra of Himachal Pradesh. The objectives of the study were: (i) to study the socio-economic characteristics of cropping pattern and non-farm income for different sizes (ii) to critically examine the problems and the constrains in the development of tribal agriculture. The sample design, adopted for the study, consisted of two stage stratified random sampling and household in the villages as the primary sampling unit and household in the villages as the secondary and ultimate sampling unit. There were 375 households in the sample frame which comprised 226 small farms (less than 2 acre) and 149 large farms (more than 2 acre). The primary data was collected on pre-tested schedules by survey method. The study reported that agriculture was the chief source of livelihood of the people of the Kinnavura as nearly 60 per cent of the total working force is engaged in agricultural pursuits. 60 per cent of the total family members were within the working age group of 16–55 yrs. Literacy among males and females was 48.84 and 33.99 per cent respectively.

The most important crop of the study area was Barley. The sample had 29.87 per cent of the gross cropped area under barley followed by 18.16 per cent under wheat. The study also reported lack of irrigation facilities, proper roads and means of communication.[63]

Regional Variation in Agriculture Development

Jairath and Santhi Sarup M.S. (1991) had conducted a study on regional variation in Agricultural development of 12 districts of Himachal Pradesh. In their study, they explained that the agricultural development ensures the increasing availability of cultivated area, irrigation, water inputs used and this spread the adoption of new agricultural technology consisting of bio-chemical and mechanical innovations. It helped in increasing the cropping intensity and thereby raising per unit production and productivity of land and labour. The study was conducted on the basis of an alternative approach, taxonomic method was utilized to construct such an index which would be able to rank different districts/regions without assuming any statistical distribution. The study reported that 50 per cent of the district had lower rate of application compared to the state average of 26 Kg./acre of gross cropped area. The main cause for agricultural backwardness of these districts were lack of irrigation facilities, lower availability of net area sown per cultivator, poor spread of HYV seeds, poor availability of infrastructure facilities like roads, power and PACS.[64]

Quality of Rural Life

Dhanesekharan K.(1991) analyzed socio-economic measures of quality of rural life. Poverty is usually measured within the framework of the minimum calories intake norm elaborated during the sixties. The point has often been made that the consumption (minimum calories) is not a completely satisfactory yardstick for measuring poverty especially when provision of minimum needs to the people is a basic objective of planning in India. It excludes not only the luxuries but also the necessary items of private and social consumption, such as housing, education, health etc. (Chaudhri, 1979, p. 185).

In the above context, an attempt has been made to evolve a new measure of poverty index, which is called as Rural Quality of life index (RQLI). The poverty index is a more scientific method, because various variables are taken into consideration in determining the poverty levels. The index evolved here was intended to identify the rural poor and to evaluate the real impact of development programmes especially when eradication of poverty (i.e. provision of minimum needs to the people)is a basic objective of planning. In view of the stress laid in Indian planning on the provision of basic needs to the people, it is important to use some such yardstick as the RQLI for assessing growth and plan performance. It is hoped that the RQLI presents the possibility of constructing valid reliable micro and macro models of rural development which can shed more light on the development process.[65]

Constraints in the Socio-economic Development of Village

Annoop Singh Dhukia and Sharma R.K. (1998) studied constraints in socio-economic development of villages. This study was taken up in Karmal, a village in Hisar district of Hariyana state to delineate the constraints in different aspects, namely, agriculture, animal husbandry, education, employment, food and nutrition, health and family welfare, housing, water supply and sanitation, street lighting and metalled street flooring, approach roads and recreational activities.

A careful attention to the constraints presented above indicated that every area of the development was ridden with problems. A closer examination of the constraints brought to surface that lack of finance and initiative on the part of either the panchayat or village people or the concerned government agency have been road blocking the desired pace of village development.

Rural development could not be self-propelling, and would surely fail in impelling the community to seek its own welfare in the absence of people's active participation. Participation might be in the form of donation or even free manual labour (Maheswari, 1985).[66]

Rural Towns

Saxena. D.P. (1994) had made a study on rural towns and socio-economic development of villages, with special reference to eastern U.P. in India. There were 244 respondents in eight sample villages. The data was collected by personal interview schedule method. The study reported that an alarming rise in the economic status had come to light especially to those who were previously below poverty line (u) up to Rs. 12,000 pa. It was also observed that joint family was found in the process of being replaced by the extended family. Yet, joint family was the dominant feature. The study also reported that the positive values were expressed more in respect of inter-caste marriage, protection to the minorities, backward castes and classes, female education, modern fashion, secularism and changing traditional centered occupations.[67]

Impact of Commutation of Varanasi City

Yadava. K.N.S. (1992) had made a survey on the impact of commutation to Varanasi city on the economy of villages in its hinterlands in 1984. Therewere 720 households in her sample frame which comprised 360 commuting and 360 non-commuting persons. Two types of schedules were used to obtain the data. There were (i) village schedule and (ii) household schedule. The data was collected by the personal interview method. Chi-square test, Z. test, Morkov transition models, percentages were used to analyze the data.

It was found that about 59 per cent commuters belong to the 'high' social status group, about 19 per cent to the very high, about 23 per cent to the 'middle' and 5 per cent to 'lower' social status group. So far as the economic status of the household is concerned, it was found that 66.39 per cent commuting households have low economic status while 75.85 per cent non-commuting households belong to this category.[68]

Agricultural Labourers

Narayana K.V. *et al* (1989), had conducted a study on the impact of development programs on a targeted group of agricultural labours in Warangal district. There were 50 sample labour households selected on random basis from a village in Warangal district. The objectives of the study were:

(i) To enquire into socio-economic status of agricultural labours in the study village.

(ii) To estimate the expenditure and net income from various schemes sanctioned to the labour households

To observe the source-wise and purpose-wise distribution or debt burden of the labour households. The study concluded that the schemes which were aimed to ameliorate the conditions of labour households resulted in deteriorating their economic conditions the debt burden of labour households increased without formation of any additional assets.[69]

Problems of Institutional Finance

Sujit Sikidan, (1988), in his article on problems of institutional finance in mill areas, explained that in order to improve the standard of living, quality of life, and to alleviate rural poverty several other schemes have to be introduced simultaneously to achieve a total development. Education , metamorphosis and social awakening with the conscious self introspection have germinated the idea of development among the planners and the hill people alike. The planning strategy intends to husband the financial outlay with scarce population of the mills adorned with diffused physical resources.[70]

Investment on Fixed Assets

Tripathi (1984-95) had examined the pace and pattern of investment of fixed assets and capital formation in agriculture. He also analyzed the extent of investment on different farm assets and its impact on capital formation. The study was based on an intensive enquiry of 60 farmers selected from six villages, two from high hills (> 1600 meters mean sea level) and two from mid hills (1000-1600) meters mean sea level and two from valley farming systems (< 1000 meters mean sea level) of the Uttar Pradesh hills using random sampling technique. The data were collected from the selected respondents at first in 1984-85 and again in 1994-95. The same set of the sample was used at two points of time. The results of the study revealed that as per farm investment on fixed farm assets excluding land, ranged from Rs. 19,525 to Rs. 24.637 in 1984-85 and from Rs. 45,395 to Rs. 58,048 in 1994-95. The performance of investment tended to increase with the increase in the elevation, but on per hectare basis it showed a reverse trend mainly due to larger size of holdings in high-hill situations. The investment on farm building ranged from Rs. 13,590 in 1984-85 Rs. 48.425 per farm in 1994-95 which tended to increase with the decrease in the altitude of the farm on per hectare basis. The investment on farm buildings increased at an annual rate of 14.4 per cent in valley farming situation from 1984-85 to 1994-95.

These findings proved that there was a deceleration in overall capital formation in real terms during 1984-85 to 1994-95 in the study area.[71]

Managing Hill Resources

Swarn Lata Arya & Mittal S.P. (1992) studied managing hill resources through community participation. The study area was confined to Shivali hills of Northern India during the last one hundred years or so has earned great concern among the departments, concerned with the management of hills and their resources .The on slaught of man and cattle has virtually left these hills completely denuded with consequent problems of severe soil erosion, sedimentation and floods. The conventional approach to rehabilitate these hills has proved futile, for the problems of grazing, illicit felling of trees, etc have continued unabated.[72]

Productivity of Resources

Sharma M.L. *et al* (1988-89) examined the economics of black gram cultivation and productivity of important resources used for it at the existing level of production technology adoption in the prevalent hill farming system.

The study concludes the need for reallocation of the input resources to reduce the loss in terms of net returns and to make the production of black gram viable at the existing level of production technology adoption and resource use in the hill farming system.[73]

Technological Change

Rajesh and Kombairaju (1999) attempted to understand the role of technological change in the economic status of female workers separately. Specifically, it attempted to analyze the female labour participation and examined the impact of technological changes in female labour employment in rain–fed agriculture.

The study found that the economic status of the female labourers remained inferior to their male counter parts in dry farming areas, although the effect of technological change seemed to be favorable on both sexes of the agricultural labour force.[74]

Environmental Protection

Pant K.P. and Pandey V.K. (1994-95) had attempted to delineate the major environmental protection objectives for the hill agriculture of Nepal and to develop a multi objective farm planning model for minimization of environmental problems while maintaining the present levels of food grains production and farm income. For the purpose, a representative hill district of Dhading in Nepal was selected for obtaining the requisite data and other information.

It was concluded that agricultural development through modern farm technology was reported to be causing several adverse environmental effects: Water run-of, carrier fertile soil. To augment soil productivity chemical fertilizers were used. These fertilizers too are carried of by rain and irrigation, polluting water bodies. The use of pesticides besides being a health hazard, which causes soil degradation through biological impoverishment of the soil much more and widespread in hill agriculture due to the fragile ecosystem and its impact is on the plains through downstream regimentation, flooding and water pollution. Cattle grazing and forest fodder lopping in the hills further accelerate the rate of soil erosion by denuding forests and pastures. It is hypothesized here that the extent of these adverse environmental effects could be considerably reduced through optimal farm planning, while meeting the present levels of subsistence.[75]

Optimum Utilization of Land Resources

Bhardwaj S.P. and Gupta H.C. (1991) had analyzed a micro level study on "optimum utilization of land resources". The availability of cultivable land has been under various pulls and pressures in our developing economy.The existing low land–man ratio will be further narrowed down in the years to come. The only option for enhancing food production lies in the vertical growth of land resources. This study was based on the survey data of sample farmers of Gurghar district, Haryana state. The study revealed that a significant proportion of the holdings in the area was unirrigated. The extent of irrigation varied from 55 per cent to 75 per cent of the gross cropped area. The existing land use pattern indicated that margined or less fertile lands were allocated to crops like barley, gram and mustard, especially by the small category of farmers.

However, the optimum land use planning showed that even in the unirrigated conditions, land can be optimally used in growing much remunerative crops like gram and mustard. The study concluded that farmers should be suitably advised to optimize the use of their land resources so that total food production can be enhanced.[76]

Energy Use

Saraswat and Prem S. Dahiya (1998) had attempted to analyze the energy use pattern on different sizes of farms in different hill zones of Himachal Pradesh, to study the economics of energy use in agriculture on different sizes of farms in different hill zones and to suggest policy measures for rational energy availability and utilization for development of hill agriculture on sustainable basis.

For the purpose of study, a sample of 150 farmers were selected from Kangra district low hills, Solan district in mid hills and Shimla district in high hills and information about the energy utilization, cost of production and returns from crops on farms were collected by survey method for the agricultural year 1995-96.

The study revealed that because of agro-climatic endowment the farming systems differed in different zones; cereals and fruit-based cropping pattern are predominant in low hills while vegetable based farming is practiced in mid hills and only fruit farming in high hills. Commercial crops were more labour and capital intensive than cereals. Human labour used was lowest in low hills to high hills. In low hills energy use was 5 times less than in mind and high mills, and bullock labour use was 2.5 times less. This was because of mechanization of low hills. Energy input cost is the highest in mid-hills because of very high labour utilization. The returns from vegetable based farming system In mid-hills was the highest as compared to the farming systems in high hills and low hills.[77]

Pattern of Energy Use in Various Agro-Eco-Systems

Tripathi R.S. (1998) had enquired into the level and pattern of energy use in various agro-eco systems and estimated the productivity of important input resource used under high hill (>1,600 meters mean sea level) and valley (<900 meters mean sea levels) farming systems of Uttara Khand region in Uttar Pradesh. In this study regression analysis was used and it indicated more than 69 per cent of the variation in energy out put in all the agro-ecosystems due to variation in energy use of the five input resources (human labour, bullock labour, seeds, manure and fertilizer) considered for the analysis. This variation ranged from 69.30 for finger millet-followed in mid hill to 94.09 per cent in pulses (mixed)-rape seed and mustard agro ecosystem of valley farming system.

The findings revealed that the average size of operational holdings was extremely small varying from 20 per cent in mid-hills to 29 per cent in the valleys with cropping intensity of

15.5 per cent. Most of the area was occupied by cereals and pulses, in addition to fruits and off-season vegetables.[78]

Factors Affecting Land Market

Ramesh Chand S.C.and Tewari had made a study on the factors affecting land market transactions and its impact on size distribution of holdings in a Hill Region in the year 1991.

This study had focused on land market transactions in mountain agriculture which is distinct from other situation. Land is the most scare resource in hill region. Due to limited investment opportunities, land is the most important asset for making private investment in such regions. This study was undertaken in this background and it aimed at examining the socio-economic factors affecting sale/purchase of agriculture land in the state of Himachal Pradesh. Factors contributed by the buyers/sellers for buying/selling of land were studied and the impact of land transactions on land owner ship pattern was analyzed. The study was conducted in Solan district, which represented mid-hill zone of the state. This study consisted of 70 sellers and 64 buyers who indulged in land transaction during the year 1990-91. It was observed that the buyers of land had 2to 3 times higher inherited land, value of wealth, off-farm income and farm income as compared to the sellers of land. The percentage of literacy was also higher in the case of buyers of households. The present study also find that the percentage of literacy was higher than the land owned people. The sellers of the land had sold their land for repaying the debt and constructing houses.[79]

Appropriate Technology

Kanta Prasad (1989), in his study on socio-economic requirements of appropriate technologies for eradication of rural poverty, suggested that the nature of technologies should be relevant for eradication of poverty and identification of the conditions necessary for their successful applications. If technology is to be a major element in poverty eradication, then its choice has to be carefully done. We have to find out what technologies are really needed for this purpose. Past experience suggests that a number of technologies that were developed as laboratory exercises could not be accepted by the potential users. There is thus need for an amendment of technologies already developed or to be developed. Specific criteria would be needed for this purpose. He also suggested that the appropriateness of technology would vary from area depending upon variations in such factors as topography and climate, living style and cultural, levels or skills and education etc.[80]

Iruvelipattu Village

Raj K.N. (1977) had conducted a study on a village in India and its political economy. He selected Iruvelipattu village in Tamil Nadu. Some of his observations about the village at the time are relevant even now. He pointed out that an Indian worker who earns very low wages , has a very low standard of expenditure and attains a very low level of efficiency, and there were three characteristics of Indian life which are so inter connected, that it is impossible to say which is cause rather than effect.[81]

Determinants of Poverty

Narayana Reddy G. (1989) in his article on Socio-Psychological Determinants of poverty, had analyzed the characteristics of poverty, determinants of poverty, socio-cultural determinants of poverty, and psychological determinants of poverty. In this article he found that the economic factors are a part of several socio-psychological factors that influence changes in poverty levels among the rural poor, factors such as low literacy level, low health status, mal-nourishment, large size of family and lack of awareness, aspiration and motivation for further development are some of the important socio-cultural and psychological determinants which play an important role in determining the position of the poor rural society. He concluded that recognizing the interplay of social factors like family structure, poverty rights, inheritance and old age.

Security, the approach of integrated action may be extended to link family planning with other programs of socio-economic development e.g., poverty, employment generation and rural and urban development.[82]

Poverty in Pathipaka Village

Sadanandam and Bhaskar G. (1989) had conducted a study on rural poverty in Pathipaka village, Warangal district, to find out the consumption expenditure of the rural poor in the village. There were 60 sample respondents in this sample frame which comprised 15 marginal farmers,15 agricultural labourers, 15 rural artisans, and 15 others. A structured questionnaire was administered to a total of 60 respondents. The study reported that the literacy level of respondents was very low. Of the 60 respondents, 44 (73.33) were illiterates. Among the literates, 16.67 per cent of the respondents had primary education and only 10 per cent had secondary education.

The study also reported that nearly 50 per cent of the expenditure was on food items consisting of cereals, 45 per cent for marginal farmers, 46 per cent for rural artisans and 50 per cent for agricultural labourers. Expenditure on education and health also formed a small proportion of the total non food expenditure. Per capita monthly consumption expenditure of the sample households was very low. The study found that the development of agro-based industries would help to utilize local resources and provide employment opportunities to the poor.[83]

Perceptions of the Poor

Sharma A.K. (1989) had conducted a socio-psychological study on what the poor think about their poverty in U.P. The study analyzed three dimensions (i.e.) the perceptions of the poor, their focus of control and how they can be developed. There ware 550 sample respondents in the sample frame, which comprised 500 poor and 50 non-poor in the selected villages of U.P.on the quota sampling method. The data was collected by structured interview schedule. The study reported that 70 per cent of the poor, the critical level of earnings, which can enable them to cross the poverty line, subjectively, was less than Rs. 1,000 but more than Rs. 500. The model category of their response was Rs. 500-700 which was quite close to the officials understanding of the poverty line.

The study also reported that an overwhelming majority of the poor (more than 80 per cent) attributed poverty to some external factors, e.g. parents, society, fate or Government policies. Only 18.77 per cent poor said that they themselves were responsible for their own poverty and only 16.80 per cent attributed general poverty to some personal factor. The study concluded that the perceptions of poverty development among poor and a few rich are very different. Many of the non-poor had involvement in economically developing the under-developed. But, in general, this participation was more in the form of personal acts of altruism, intended to help some people, individually. It can even be a political act of helping "their own people" against owners .It does not bring about change in the social structure as such.[84]

Conceptual Consideration of Poverty

G.C. Kar (1989), in his article, on conceptual considerations of poverty, wrote that the poverty eradication programmes, so far, have been thought of or implemented through two set of economic measures, viz., those directed towards provision of employment opportunities and income generating assets to the strategies and their success depended squarely on the extent of relative deprivation in the poverty scale. Creation and transfer of income generating asset to the poor would not alleviate poverty. Poverty alleviation programme, therefore, should take note of the capabilities of the target population with regard to asset management. If for some reasons, asset creation is preferred to job-creation on the poverty alleviation strategy, a blending of both can be made by resorting to a group-oriented action plan.[85]

Trends in Rural Poverty

Bhaskar G. (1994), in his book on, Trends in Rural Poverty, explained that mass poverty is a situation where a large percentage of population suffers from a chronic shortage of food and other basic needs like clothing, housing, medical, and educational facilities and hence victims of ill-health, disease, sheer animal hunger, reduced longevity and ignorance which is an obvious phenomenon in any third world country. The tragedy of contemporary mass poverty in the South is much more staggering in its dimensions than that of developed countries in their entire history of economic development that the pace of economic development in the developing nations is much slower than that of developed countries in the corresponding historical phase, of its industrialization. Therefore, mass poverty in the developing countries is not simply a matter of the microeconomic theory of economic growth involving econometric models of the factors and conditions of economic growth, without any reference to historical structures.[86]

Social Security

Vasanthi K. (2000), in her article on poverty and social insecurity, analyzed the genesis of the antipoverty schemes in India, their multiplicity, their past achievements and highlights as to how certain essential organizational and financial aspects have to be incorporated for its success. She reported that poverty is a multi-dimensional complex and needs to be understood not only in economic terms but also from the point of technological advances. Removal of poverty alleviation programs invariably lose their effectiveness due to leakages.[87]

Micro Level Planning

Ganesh (1985), in his article on Micro Level Plan for Rural Development, had analysed various plans for rural development. He explained that in India, development planning is the accepted tool to achieve socio-economic development of the masses, steeped in poverty, illiteracy and deprived of freedom of mobility by institutional constraints. He also indicated that the micro level planning is a competent concept to help the unemployed and the people living below the poverty line. It's main purpose as already stated, is to accelerate the process of decentralization in the hope that more systematic planning effort with a smaller coverage will not only help speed up the development process, but also improve it qualitatively.[88]

Agricultural Growth and Rural Development

Thamarajakshi R. (1989), in her article, on Agricultural Growth, Rural Development and Employment Generation, reported that the poverty alleviation, employment generation and human resource development were principal goals in the developing economics of Asia. Rural poverty was a larger issue than unemployment, for real earnings of the rural workforce depend not merely on their employment–unemployment status, but more specifically, on the quantum of employment, their participation rates, the nominal wages and price level of consumption goods purchased by rural labourers. Removal of unemployment itself cannot eradicate poverty and have, therefore, to go beyond employment programs and should focus on agricultural production and rural development.[89]

Science, Technology and Eradication of Rural Poverty

Bal Dev Singh (1988), in his article, on science, Technology and Eradication of Rural poverty, described that in the developing countries, several desirable objectives stand in contradiction with each other. High level of mechanization and automation may achieve higher productivity and efficiency but create unemployment. He suggested that poverty and more particularly rural poverty as a social phenomenon is not a political social phenomenon. There are groups and interests in the system that benefit from unemployment and keep others backward and in poverty. Unless there is political will to change the state of affairs, neither planning nor science and technology can do much. India is country of great degree of social, economic and cultural diversity. Plans for eradication of poverty could more appropriately be drawn at a state level. The question remains whether the political leadership at a state level has the political will and in some cases the necessary management and administrative competence to plan and carry through the programmes.[90]

The studies reviewed above are either partial or concerned about one or two aspects of the life of the rural and hill people. But, the present study is comprehensive as it deals with the origin and settlement of the people in Palamathi Hills, their socio-economic conditions, extent of poverty and the development programs undertaken in the hill. Thus it differs from the previous studies. The present study is first of its kind to be undertaken in Palamathi Hills and it would add to the existing knowledge on the subject.

NOTES

1. Cooling Wood de (1983), 21 Century Universal Encyclopedia", Vol. 26, Regency Publishing, Sydney, p. 49.
2. Harish Chandra Singh, (1989) "Rural Environment Development and Planning", Chugh Publications, Allahabad, p. 122.
3. James M., Rubenstein, *et al.* (1990), "The Cultural Land Scape-An Introduction to Human Geography". Prentice Hall of India, New Delhi, pp. 342-344.
4. John Black (1997), "A Dictionary of Economics", Oxford University Press, New York, p. 229.
5. Gohcheng and Gillian C. Morgan (1988), "Human and Economic Geography". Oxford University Press, Oxford, p. 33.
6. Paramjit Kaurchawhan (1998), "Migration of Women Labour and their Problems", Southern Economist, Vol. 37 (15), p. 9.
7. Agarwala. S.N. and Singha. V.P. (1901) "Indian Population Problems". Tata MC-Graw Hill, New Delhi, p. 217.
8. Kingsly Davis (1995), "Human Society" Surjeet Publications". Delhi, p. 590.
9. Kingsly Davis (1947), "Future Migration into Latin America". Milk Bank Memorial Fund Quarterly, Vol. 25, pp. 44, 62.
10. I bid, pp. 208, 211.
11. The World Book Encyclopedia (1959), Chicago, Field Enterprises Educational Corporation, Merchandise Martplaya. Vol. 8, p. 3421.
12. Ronald Boyce. R., *op.cit*, p. 56.
13. Dubey, *op cit*, p. 106.
14. Mamoria, C.B. (1981) "Social Problems and Social Disorganization in India". Kitabmahal, Allahabad, pp. 270,271.

15. Rai. B.C. (1988), "Education and society–a study of sociological foundation of education"
16. Mosby Medical Encyclopedia,(1992) Published in New York City, p. 360.
17. Park J.E. and K. Park (1991), Park's Text Book of Preventive and Social Medicine". Banarsidas Bharat Publishers Jabalpur, p. 12.
18. Ngugi. D.N., P.K. Karau, *et.al* (1992), "East African Agriculture". Macmillan, London, p. 216.
19. Ibid, p. 330.
20. John Black, *op.cit*, p.15.
21. Arulanandam and Raman K.S. (2002), "Advanced Accountancy". Himalaya Publishing House, Delhi, p. 67.
22. Arockiasamy (1981), "Economic Analysis". Shanthi Publishing House, Tirunelveli, p. 183.
23. James M. Rubenstein and Robert S. Bacon (1990), "The cultural Land scape-An Introduction to Human Geography". Prentice-Hall of India, New Delhi, pp. 41,42.
24. Desai A.R. (1969), "Rural Sociology in India". Popular Prakasam, Bombay, pp. 26, 27.
25. Ruddar Datt and Sundharam K.P.M. (2001), "Indian Economy" S. Chand & Company". New Delhi, p. 469.
26. Kurnati Lingaiah (1991), "Dictionary of Economics". Link Publications, Bharatpur, p. 21.
27. Sadhu and Singh (1986), "Fundamentals of Agricultural Economics". Himalaya Publishing House, Bombay, p. 252.
28. Ibid, p. 252.
29. Karnati Lingaiah, *Op. cit*, p. 67.
30. John Black, *Op. cit*, p. 163.
31. Ghodake. N.B. (1986), "Encyclopedic Dictionary of Economics," Volume 5, Mittal Publications, New Delhi, pp. 640, 641.
32. Arockiasamy, *op.cit*, p. 132.
33. John Black, *op.cit,* p. 36.
34. Peter B. Nortoan and Joseph J. (1994), "The New Encyclopaedia Britannica Inc", Vol. 9 Esposito President, Pub. Group, Chicago, p. 652.
35. Paul A. Samuelson and William D. Nordhans (1995), "Economics", Mc Graw-Hill, Inc, New York, p. 362.

36. Varma, S.C. (1984), "Millions in Poverty grip", Kunji Publishing House, New Delhi, p. 15.
37. Rowntree B.S. (1902) "Poverty–a study of turn life", Macmillan, London, PXVII.
38. Wilbur G.L. (ed) (1973) "Poverty–a new perspective" the University Press of Kentucky, Lexington, p. 6.
39 Desai S.S.M. (1986), "Fundamentals of Rural Economics" Himalaya Publishing House, Bombay, p. 120.
40. ICSSR (1981), "Social Science Research and the problem of poverty", 1st Nat. conference on Social Sci, New Delhi Vol. 1 No. 2 & 3, p. 42.
41. IASSI (1985), "Demographic perspective in Poverty", Vol. 4, p. 5.
42 Karnati Lingaih, op, p. 133.
43 Dewett, K.K. *etal*, (2000),"Indian Economics", S. Chand & Company, New Delhi, p. 445.
44. Vaish (2002), "Macro Economic Theory". Vikas Publishing House, New Delhi, pp. 155, 156.
45. Grewal (1985), "Rural Economics". Kalyani Publishers, New Delhi p. 82.
46. Ibid, p. 83.
47. Charles P. Kindleberger & Bruce Herrick (1958), "Economic Development", Mc-Graw Hill, Chicago Inc, p. 2.
48 Meier & Baldwin (1976), "Economic Development Theory, History, Policy" Asia publishing house New Delhi, p. 2.
49. The World Book Encyclopedia (1959), Chicago, Field Enterprises Educational Corporation, Merchandise Mart playa. Volume 8, p. 3421.
50. Ruddar Datt, op cit, p. 86.
51. Mahajan V.S. (I990), "Agriculture & Rural Economy in India", Deep & Deep Publications, New Delhi, p. 350.
52. Dulhashi, P.R. (1997), "Potentialities and Limitations of Co-operations for integrated Rural Development". Co-operative News Digest, Vol. XXVIII, (5), p. 68.
53. "Harijan" (1936), Selection from Gandhi", p. 71.
54. Spencer Hatch D. (1936), "Up from Poverty in India", Oxford University Press, Madras, pp. 184, 185, 186.
55. Sadhukhan. S.K. (1982), "Economic Geography". An Appraisal of Resources, S. Chand & Company New Delhi, p. 11.

56. Anon, (1996), "Social Forestry Schemes". Council for Advancement of peoples Action and Rural Technology, Bengal offset works, New Delhi, p. 1.

57. Khanna. K.K. and Gupta V.K. (1994), "Economic and Commercial Geography". Sultan Chand & sons, New Delhi, p. 10.1.

58. K. Padmanaban (1997), "Economic Transition with a human face", I.I.P.A, Tirupattur local branch, pp. 1-12.

59. Carr–Harris J. (ed.) (1995), "Mountain and people"–A peoples Perspective from the Indian Himalayas". Sri Bhuvaneswari–Mahila Ashram. Paper Presented at the NGO Consultation Sustainable Development, Lima, pp. 19, 20.

60. E. Nagabushana Rao (1989), "Planning units for Rural Development–a study", Kurukshetra, Vol. XXXVII, (6), pp. 49,50.

61. Udaya Bhaskara Reddy (1986), "Socio-Economic conditions of the rural poor", Kurukshetra, Vol. XXIV, (60), pp.18-20.

62. Balbir Kumar & Karam Singh (1992), "Socio–Economic Problems of Tribal Gujjars in Punjab". IASSI Quarterly, Vol. II, pp. 157-161.

63. Oberal, R.C. and Chandal B.S. *et al.* (1993), "Socio-Economic status and constraints of Tribal Economy, Kinnaura of Himachal Pradesh", IASS Quarterly Vol. No. 122, pp.173-175.

64. M.S. Jairath and Santhi Sarup (1991), Regional variation in Agricultural development, Agricultural situation in India. Vol. XXXIVI, (9), New Delhi, pp. 15-17.

65. Dhanasekharan, K. (1991), "Socio-Economic Measures of Quality of Rural Life". An alternative approach for measures of Rural poverty. "Indian Journal of Agricultural Economics Vol.XLVI, (1), pp. 31-43.

66. Anoop Singh, Dhukia and Sharma R.K. (1998),"Constraints in Socio-Economic Development of Village". Kurukshetra, Vol. 46, (9) pp. 28-30.

67. Saxena D.P. (1994) "Rural Towns and Socio-Economic Development of Villages, with special reference to Eastern U.P" Mital Publications, New Delhi, pp. 27-29.

68. Yadava K.N.S. (1992), "Rural Urban Commutation and Rural Development", Shipra Publications, New Delhi, pp.141-153.

69. Narayaṇa K.V., Ram Reddy M. *et al.* (1989), "Development Schemes for Rural Poor". Kurukshetra, Vol. 37(7), pp. 43-45.

70. Sujit Sikidan (1988), "Problems of Institutional Finance in Hill areas", Kurukshetra, Vol. 37 (3), pp. 26-29.

71 Tripathi R.S. (1996), "Pattern of investment of Fixed Assets and Capital Formation in Different subsistence Hill Farming Systems of Uttar Pradesh", Indian Journal of Agricultural Economics, Vol. 51, (4), pp. 626, 627.

72. Swarn Lata Arya & Mittal S.P. (1992) "Managing Hill Resources thro' community Participation". Kurukshetra Vol XL, (4), pp. 15-18.

73. Sharma M.L. and Jagadish Kumar, *et al.* (1993) "Cost and Return Analysis of Black gram (*Phaseolus mungo*) in Uttar Pradesh Hills", Indian Journal of Agricultural Economics, Vol. XLVIII, pp. 430, 431.

74. Rajesh R. and Kombairaju S. (1999), "Impact of Technological change on Women employment in Dry Land Agriculture". Indian Journal of Agricultural Economics, Vol, 54, (2), pp. 302, 303.

75. Pant K. and Pant V.K. (1999), "Minimizing Environmental Problems in Hill Agriculture of Nepal through Multi Objective Farm Planning" Indian journal of Agriculture Economics, Vol. 54, (4), pp.79-83.

76. Bhrwaj S.P. & Guptha H.C. (1991) "A Optimum Utilization of Land Resources" Indian Journal of Agriculture Economics Vol. 46, (3), pp. 384, 385.

77. Saraswat S.P. and Prem S. Dahiya (1998), "Pattern and Economics of Energy use in Hill Agriculture, a case of Himachal Pradesh", Indian Journal of Agriculture Economics, Vol. 53, (3), pp. 310.

78. Tripathi R.S. (1998), "Level of Energy use in the Hill farming system of Uttrakhand", Indian Journal of Agriculture Economics, Vol. 53, (3), pp. 20, 281.

79. Ramesh Chand and Tewari S.C. (1991), "Factors Affecting Land–Market Transactions and its impact on size distribution of holdings in Hill Region". Indian Journal of Agricultural Economics, Vol YLVI, (3), pp. 365.

80. Kanta Prasad (1989), "Socio–Economic requirements or Appropriate Technologies for Eradication of Rural Poverty". IASSI, Quarterly Journal, Vol. 8 (i) pp. 65-71.

81. Raj K.N. (1977), "Village India and its Political Economy". University of Madras, pp. 1-12.

82. Narayana Reddy G. (1989), "Socio-Psychological Determinants of poverty". Journal of Rural Development".Vol. 8 (4), pp. 371-379.

83. A. Sadanadam and G. Bhakar (1989), "Concept of Rural Poverty". Kurukshetra, Vol. 37 (12), pp. 39-43.

84. Sharma A.K. (1989), "What the poor Think About Their Poverty". A Socio–psychological Study". The Indian Journal of Social Work,Vol. 50(2), Pp.171-181.

85. G.C. Kar (1989), "Conceptual Considerations on Poverty". Journal of Rural Development, Vol. 8 (3), pp. 1-7.

86. Bhaskar G. (1994), "Trends in Rural Poverty", RBSA Publication, Jaipur, pp.1-7.

87. Vasanthi K. (2000), "Poverty an Social Insecurity". Kurukshetra, Vol. 48, (8), pp. 46-48.

88. Ganesh A. (1985), "Micro Level plan for Rural Development". Kurukshetra, Vol. 33 (5), pp. 30, 31.

89. R.Thamarajakshi (1939), "Agricultural Growth, Rural Development and Employment Generation", Economic and Political Weekly, Vol. XXVI,(12), pp. A.5-A.8.

90. Bal Dev Singh (1988), "Science Technology and Eradication of rural poverty", IASSI Quarterly Bulletin, Vol. 72 (23), pp. 83-86.

3

DESCRIPTION OF THE STUDY AREA

INTRODUCTION

Nearly one third of the land area in India is covered by hills. Hence , hills provide livelihood to 20 to 25 per cent of the people in India. Hills are the major source of ecological stability and sustenance to innumerable species of flora and fauna. Man depends on the hill both directly and indirectly for his survival. Man draws wood and a host of other products from the hills for his use as well as for sale. Hills indirectly help man by bringing rain and by maintaining ecological balance. Thus, the study of the hill economy and its features will bring about the relationship between man and the hill.

In order to understand the socio-economic conditions of the inhabitants of the Palamathi hill, it is indispensable to discover the physical features, resources available, infrastructures and social and economic institutions of the area and the development programs undertaken, production condition etc. The description of the study area specifically deals with population, literacy, nature of occupation, religion, crop pattern, rainfall, soil and irrigation, land utilization, and several developmental schemes viz., Vellore Social Forestry Scheme , Jawahar Rozgar Yojana, Indira Memorial housing Scheme, Finance Commission, subsidy for works, State Financial commission, Employment Guarantee Scheme, underdeveloped panchayat scheme, equalization and motivation subsidy finance and establishment of tourism development, Parliamentary constituency development fund, Namaku namay thitam, Drought prone Area program etc. form the infrastructure of the area of study.

LOCATION

The area under study i.e. Palamathi and encircling area are in Vellore block of Vellore taluk, in Vellore district, of the Tamil Nadu state. It lies 15 Km east of Vellore town and covers an area of 112 sq miles. Generally, this is an area having a natural disconnection with the common terrain. At the foot of the hill lies the Kanniyambadi block. The Palamathi reserve forest and the Vellore reserve forest bisect the village from Vellore town. The study area is bounded by Vellore reserve forest and a small range of hills, which is residual in nature and said to be as Vellore hills, and is bounded by Palamathi reserve forest. On the east it is bounded by Punganur reserve forest, on the west it is bounded by Sankaranpalayam and on the north by Kodakikuppammalai and Punganur reserve forest. On the south, it is bounded by Palamathi and Punganur reserve forest.

The Location of the Palamathi Hills can be viewed in the map placed in Fig. 1.

Fig. 1: Location of Palamathi Hills in Vellore District

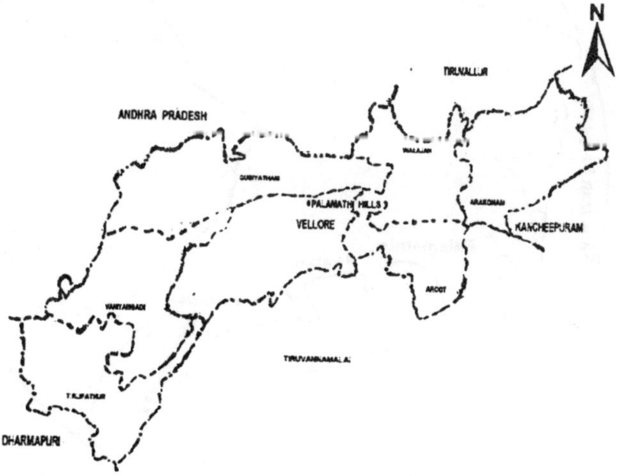

ADMINISTRATIVE SET UP

Under the administrative set up, the study area is the border village of Vellore taluk on the one hand and a strait to the Walajapet taluk on the other hand .The Palamathi area falls under the Survey of India Topography sheet 57 P/1. The exact geographical co-ordinates are North Latitude 12^0 52 40^2 and East longitude 79^0 10/503 .

The hamlets are administered by the Village Administrative Officer (VAO), whose office is located at Palamathi. The VAO, whose office is located at Palamathi, is under the control of Tahasildar and the Collector of the Vellore District. The location of the five hamlets in the Palamathi Hills is presented in Fig. 2. The Palamathi Hills comes under the Vellore Panchayat Union, the location of the Palamathi Hills in the Block and its contours are presented in Fig. 2.

Fig. 2: Hamlets in Palamathi Hills

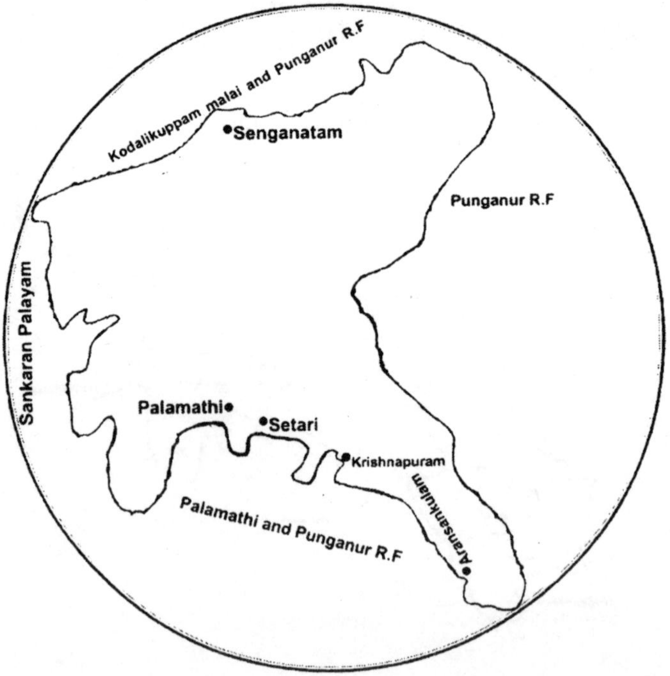

Fig. 3: Vellore Panchayat Union Map

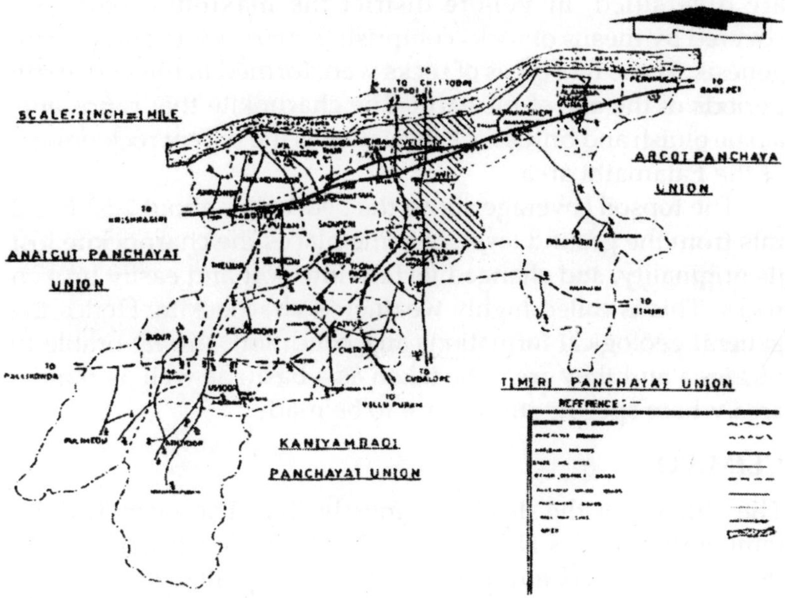

TOPOGRAPHY

The physiography of the Palamathi Hills is unique. This controlled basin type of area is located in the midst of smaller hills and reserved forest. Though the Vellore District has its own hill ranges on the Western Ghats, which leads to the Eastern Ghats series, the present study area exists in an isolated patch of smaller residual hills broken in the Baramahal range of hills that starts from the neighbouring state of Andhra Pradesh. Under Topology, this is an undulated terrain. The elevation differences are peculiar and considerable. Since it is located in a valley at strait portion of the reserve forest area, the triangulation height of this study area is 567.9 meter from mean sea level.

GEOLOGY

Geology of an area is the most wanted criteria for knowing anything about the past and present status. In Tamil Nadu, the geological formations and its structural textural features are diversified. In Vellore district the maximum parts are covered by means of rocks comprising charnockite and granite genesis. These two types of rocks were formed in the very early periods of the age of the earth. The charnokite that represents a pale bluish and brittle rock formation is the parent rock unique of the Palamathi area.

The topsoil coverage above the bedrock is about 1.52 to 3.2 mts from the ground level. In some places the charnockite lost its originality, and changed its face into soft and easily broken rocks. This is called highly weathered charnockite. Hence the general geological formations and conditions are favorable to this area and they are to be taken as a basin as well as remote area where specific studied are to be made.

CLIMATE

The climate of the district is mostly dry. The normal daily temperature raises slowly in the mid-day but it gets cooled down and the maximum temperature would fall in the evening. Notable maximum temperature ranges between 18.9^0 C. to 40.9^0 C. The hot summer of this area is up to the month of May and it ranges from 23·8^{0}C to 40.9^{0}C. This is because the Vellore Temperature station is very near to the study area and therefore temperatures are the same.

PRECIPITATION

Considering the general rainfall pattern of the nation, the average rainfall of the study area unto the Vellore district is optimum. The mean annual rainfall is contributed by the seasonal rainfall of (1) South West monsoon and (2) North East monsoon. The un-seasonal and transitional rainfall is also contributing to some extent to the total rainfall.

The monsoon rainfall attains its peak during October and November. The different monthly average rainfall for the period 2002 is appended herewith in Table 1. Over and all, the rainfall noted in this district is insufficient. This can be promoted by means of vegetating the barren lands vastly available in the hillock and inhabitant area.

Table 1
Normal Rainfall in Vellore District During the Year 2002
(As per District Statistical Hand book)

Sl. No.	*Climate*	*Weather*	*Month*	*Rainfall Received (mm)*	*Average rainfall (mm)*
1.	Normal	Winter	January	0.6	0.66
			February	-	
2.	Normal	Hot	March	-	18.1
			April	6.6	
			May	11.5	
3.	Monsoon	South West	June	32.70	93.26
			July	20.00	
			August	26.24	
			September	14.32	
4.	Monsoon	North East	October	6.85	42.47
			November	13.61	
			December	22.01	

Source: Metrological Observatory, Fort Vellore-4.

DRAINAGE

As far as the study area is concerned, this falls in Vellore minor basin of the major basin of the River Palar. There are no specific small dams for this area as it is encircled by the reserve forest and small hillocks along the three sides that serves as small basin. The main source of water supply to this area is rainfall and very little amount of water is drained from the hills surrounding during the rainy seasons. As the slope of Palamathi area is towards South and South West, the general flow pattern of the area is in accordance with the slope of the terrain.+

IRRIGATION

For agricultural purpose, there are 139 open wells of which 9 wells are not used for irrigation, 103 pump sets, 32 oil engines, four overhead tanks, one ground level water tank, four drinking water wells and 23 bore wells. The remaining area is irrigated by ponds, small canals and rain water. The area of study is not

+ Soil Atlas, Vellore District soil survey and land use organization, Dept of Agriculture, Tamil Nadu, Vellore–1988, Pg 38-48.

connected with irrigational structures. There is no adequate supply of surface water to the public of the Palamathi.*

SOIL

Soil is the geological residue and it is the prime and vital criteria for the development of a region. Important soil types found in this district are red ferruginous loam and sandy loam. Black soil is generally limited to the Palar, Ponnaiyar and Cheyyar river basins, as also to the adjacent areas of a few large irrigation tanks.

Gudiyatham, Walajah, Arakonam, Cheyyar and Vellore have clayey soil of the black series. While clayey soil is deemed more fertile than the loam, higher grades of black loams are better for crops. The red series sand is generally found all over the district, and it is predominant in the taluks of Tiruvanamalai, Chengam and Wandiwash.

In Palamathi hills, there are two kinds of soil viz., Kolathur series (Kol) and Mangalathupathy series, the description of which are explained in the following paragraphs.

Kolathur Series

The description of the Kolathur series is given below:

AP 0.12 cm dark brown (10YR 3/3) Sandy clay; moderate medium sub angular blocky; slightly hard(dry) slightly firm (moist) slightly sticky and slightly plastic (wet) common fine roots;common fine pores; clear smooth boundary, slow permeability, pH 7.0. Bt 1 21-74cm, dark brown (1.5 Yr. ¾) clay; strong medium sub-angular blocky hard (dry) firm moist, sticky and plastic(wet) small irregular, soft, iron concretions , patchy and thick clay films, slow permeability, pH 6.9, 74 cm, weathered genesis.

Mangalathupathy Series

The description of the mangalathupathy series is given below:

0.47 yellowish red (5YR4/6) loamy sand; loose (dry) friable (moist) common fine roots, rapid permeability, clear smooth

* District Statistical Office, Vellore District Census Book, 2001.

boundary; pH 7.6, 93.103 cm red (2.5 YR 4/6), sandy dry loam sub angular blocky. Slightly hard (dry) slightly firm (moist few fine roots) fine pores: slow permeability; diffused boundary pH 7.6, 103-133 cm, weathered genesis.

GROUND WATER

The water requirements at Palamathi hills are met by the surface and the ground water. The quantum of surface water can be measured from its flow and storage, whereas the quantum in respect of ground water is measured in terms of water levels. The water level or the occurrence of ground water under the sub-surface condition is measured as the depth to the water table. If the water level is nearer to the surface, the water will be more, if it crosses deeper, the area will be dry.

In the Palamathi hills , the water level ranges between 7m to 7.5m. The behavior of water level in some agricultural wells from this area shows a periodical lowering or down fall in the progressive summer from winter water level.[#]

LAND USE PATTERN

The total area of the village is 10.55.89 hectare. The total reserved forest area is 405.10.5 hectare. The total area of wetland is 340.71-0 ha, that includes 255.49 ha of irrigated area. The total area of dry land is 283.4ha, government porambokku land is 48.44 ha, allotted government land for building houses is 4.87 hectare, wasteland is 378.37 hectare, swamp area is 238.040 and many time irrigated area is 67.78.

AREA UNDER IMPORTANT CROPS

Varieties of crops are cultivated on the agricultural farms of the people. They include food crops and non-food crops. But most of the crops in this region are rain–fed crops. Total area under different crops and irrigated area are mentioned below:

Paddy (*Oryza sativa*) 68.915 ha, Cholam (*Sorghum vulgare*) 33.89 ha, Ragi (*Eluceine corocana*) 3.665 ha, Dhal (*Vicia faba*) 19.760 ha, Black gram (*Phaseolus mungo*) 2.11.0 ha, Cow pea

---

\# Public Works Department, Vellore. 4.

Table 2
Allocation of Land

Sl. No	*Allocation of Land*	*Total area (hectares)*
1.	Wet land Irrigated land	255.49
	Many time irrigated land	85.22
2.	Dry land	283.5
3.	Government land Porambokku land	48.44
4.	Allotted government land for building houses	4.87
5.	Wasteland	378.37
6.	Reserve forest	405.10.5
7.	Area sown	238.040
8.	Area sown more than once	67.78

Source: District Statistical office, Vellore-9.

(*Vigna catjang*) 3.95 ha, Horse gram (*Dolichus biflorus*) 1.060 ha, **SPICES:** Turmeric (*Curcuma longa*) 6.470 ha, Chillie (*Capsicum annum*) 3.850 ha, **VEGETABLES:** Brinjal (*Solanum melangena*) 12.660 ha, Tomato (*Lycopersicon esculantum*) 1.760 ha, Ladies finger (*Hibiscus esculenta*) 0.400ha, Colocassia (*Colocasia antiquorum*) 3.830 ha, Yam (*Dioscorea bulbifera*) 0.100 ha **FRUITS:** Banana (*Musa paradisica*) 9.300 ha, Mangoes (*Mangifera indica*) 3.770 ha, Grapes (*Vitis vinifera*) 0.400ha, Groundnut (*Arachis hypogea*) 4.505 ha, Oilseeds 78.92 ha, Jasmine (*Trachelospermum asiaticum*) 6.830 ha, non consumable crops 305.820 hectares. The area under important crops are presented in table 3.

Table 3
Crops Cultivated

Sl. No.	*Crops cultivated*	*Area of land (ha)*
I	**Cereals**	
1.	Paddy	68.915
2.	Cholam	33.2
3.	Cambu	34.89
4.	Ragi	3.665
II	**Pulses**	
5.	Dhal	19.760
6.	Black gram	2.11.0
7.	Mochai	5.580

Sl. No.	*Crops cultivated*	*Area of land (ha)*
8.	Cow pea	3.595
9.	Horse gram	1.060
III	**Spices**	
10.	Turmeric	6.47
11.	Chillie	3.850
IV	**Vegetables**	
12.	Bringal	12.660
13.	Tomoto	1.760
14.	Colocassia	3.830
15.	Yam	0.100
16.	Ladies finger	0.400
V	**Fruits**	
17.	Banana	9.300
18.	Mango	3.770
19.	Grapes	0.400
VI	Oilseeds	
20.	Ground nut	4.505
21.	Oil seeds	78.92
VII	**Non-food crops**	
22.	Jasmine	6.830
23.	Non consumable crops	305.820

Source: District Statistical Office, Vellore-9.

POPULATION

According to 2001 census the total human population of the village was 1,886 people of which 973 people were males and 913 people were females. The schedule caste and schedule tribe population accounted for 164. Since 1951 to 2001 census the birth of male child was higher than the female child as listed in the following table 4 that indicates the decadal growth of population in Palamathi hills.

Birth and Death Rate

In the Palamathi hill village the birth and death rate of males and females are inversely proportional to each other. The birth and death rate of male was found to be higher than the female, while the birth and death of female was lower than the male. Table 5 shows the relation ship of birth and death rate of Palamathi hills.

Table 4
Decadal Growth of Population in Palamathi Hills

Sl. No.	Year	Male	Female	Total
1.	1951	424	376	800
2.	1961	494	478	972
3.	1971	564	568	1132
4.	1981	757	774	1531
5.	1991	807	802	1609
6.	2001	973	913	1886

Source: District Statistical office, Vellore-9.

Table 5
Birth and Death Rate

Sl. No	Year	Birth		Death	
		Male	Female	Male	Female
1.	1993	17	14	5	7
2.	1994	19	8	9	4
3.	1995	13	11	4	4
4.	1996	16	18	6	2
5.	1997	17	14	7	4
6.	1998	13	14	5	4
7.	1999	21	18	11	3
8.	2000	19	17	9	6
9.	2001	16	19	10	10
10.	2002	13	11	10	9
	Total	164	144	64	49

Source: Palamathi Village Panchayat Office and Child Care Center.

Literacy

Literacy level is an important socio-economic indicator of growth in any community. Recorded data and the literacy level of Palamathi people since 1951-2001 revealed that literacy was as low as 7.25% among males and 0.63% among females in the year 1951. After a decade, the per centage of male literacy level decreased by 0.67% while female literacy level increased to 2.37%. After another decade viz., in 1971 literacy level of both male and female increased tremendously. Male literacy doubled from the previous decade to 15.11%, while female literacy tripled to 7.86%. In the year 1981, literacy level fell to tremendous extent in the females giving a value of 3.92% . Male literacy level diminished slightly to the extent of 14.63%. Ever since 1991, male literacy had risen to 21.01% and it rose to 34.09% in 2001. The female literacy on the other hand in 1991 was 13.11%. After a decade, it increased to 17.60%. However, it is worth mentioning that the female literacy was lesser than the male literacy level. The details of this area is provided in the following Table 6 indicates the decadal growth of literacy in Palamathi Hills.

Table 6
Decadal Growth of Literacy in Palamathi Hills

Sl. No.	*Year*	*Male*	*Female*	*Total per cent*	
				Male	*Female*
1.	1951	58	5	7.25	0.63
2.	1961	64	23	6.58	2.37
3.	1971	171	89	15.11	7.86
4.	1981	224	60	14.63	3.92
5.	1991	338	211	21.01	13.11
6.	2001	643	332	34.09	17.60

Source: District Statistical Office Vellore-9.

Occupational Classification

According to 2001 census the occupational classification of these people: 208 were male cultivators, 30 were female cultivators, 222 were male agricultural labourers, 14 were female agricultural labourers, 4 males were involved in household industry manufacturing process, 52 males were marginal workers and 75 females were marginal workers. Total male and female workers were 486 and 119 people respectively. Unemployed males and females were 332 and 749 respectively. The following table 7 lists out the occupational classification.

HISTORY OF PALAMATHI HILL VILLAGE

Palamathi was inhabited by the people of the surrounding places. Lands were purchased and vacant lands were occupied. They indulged in the cattle rearing and agricultural activities. Transport was not available and it impeded their development. Therefore, they built their house near their cultivating lands.

Table 7
Occupational Classification in Palamathi Hills 2001

Sl. No.	*Occupation*	*Male*	*Female*
1.	Cultivation	208	30
2.	Agricultural labour	222	14
3.	Household industry	4	-
4.	Marginal worker	52	75
5.	Total workers	486	119
6.	Unemployed	332	749

Source: Palamathi Village Panchayat Office and Child Care Center.

In 1930, four important families inhabited the place. They included Narayasamy Gounder, Narayana Gounder, Potha Mandiri, Mottai mandiri.They lived in huts with thatched roofs at the foothills. They lived as joint families. They used cow dung and leaves as manure for plants. In the beginning they used water for irrigation with the help of buffaloes and ox's. Later in 1970's, they made use oil engines to draw water for the fields.

In 1975 they began to use chemical manure as fertilizers for the field. They also began to use insecticides and pesticides to some crops from diseasing. From 1980's onwards they began to live in houses made of tiles roof and asbestos roof. Today, there are many houses built with concrete roofing in Palamathi.

Palamathi during ancient times, was rich in flora and fauna. Therefore, the cattle grazing grounds were lush and green providing good fodder to the cattle. It is believed that these well grazed cattle used to rest on the rocks. When the moon would rise the milk would drip down from the udder of the cattle. Therefore, it got a literal name *Palmathi (Pal-milk, Mathi-moon).* With time, the name was transformed to Palamathi.

The Palamathi hill village is located on the Vellore highways at approximately 15 k.m distance. During the early days of 1885 this place was dense covering an area of 3,302.27 hectare of reserve forest.

Tiger, hyena, wild porcupine, wild boar, wild cats, monkeys, hare mammals, different types of snakes like king cobra, python, vipers, reptiles, eagles, wild fouls, parrots, quail, and a variety of wild species of animals were found. The flora included sandal wood tree, teakwood tree, neemtree, rose wood tree, babooltree, venkai, etc.

HISTORY OF SOCIAL AND ECONOMIC CHANGE:

Wages

Labourers who worked in the field were paid wages. The wages given to males and females differed. This is depicted in the following table 8.

Table 8
Wages for Labourers

Sl. No.	*Year*	*Wages in Rupees*	
		Male	*Female*
1.	1935-50	0.50	0.25
2.	1951-65	2.50	1.50
3.	1966-80	15.00	10.00
4.	1981-97	50.00	30.00
5.	1998-03	70.00	50.00

Source: Bagayam Range Social Forest Division, Vellore–1.

The year-wise change in wage pattern is depicted in table 8. The 1951 census records the total population of Palamathi hills to be 800, while the 2001 census records the population to be 1886, which accounts to an increase of one thousand and eighty six people (1086).

Housing

The study also observed the change in the type of roofing with change in years. This is recorded in table 9.

Table 9
Types of Houses

Sl. No	*Year*	*House type*
1.	1935-65	Thatched and Kutcha roof
2.	1966-80	Tile roof
3.	1980-97	Concrete roof

Source: Village Panchayat, Palamathi Hills.

Family Structure

People lived in joint family during the year 1935-65.After the year 1981, we see that people live as nuclear family. This shows the change in the pattern of living. According to the recent census, it is found that there is a high increase in the population when compared to the previous years.

Method of Cultivation

It was observed that from the year 1935-1979, people used the technique of hoe culture or plough culture to plough the field. From 1980's, the agro cultural practice shifted to the use of tractors to till the land. Technology has reached the village and they feel that it is affordable while few people still use ox to till their land.

Irrigation

In early times i.e. during the year,1935-51 people used ox to draw water from the wells for irrigation. But from 1951 onwards, people used pump set. After 1966, people used oil engines to draw water for irrigation.

Fertilizers

People used natural manure like cow dung, goat dung for the fields in the early years from 1935-1965. After 1966, they started to combine chemical manure along with natural manure for fertilizing crops.

Insecticides

In early 1935 to 1965, people did not use insecticides. After 1936, people began to use insecticides. After 1981, the awareness of using insecticides increased and people began to use it as pesticides.

Mode of Transport

People used to carry loads on their heads when they traveled from place to place to sell goods during the early years from 1935-1965. After 1966 people began to use bullock carts. From

1974 onwards people started to use different modes viz., bus, van and cycles for transportation. Bullock carts are used in very less number now a days.

Fuel

Firewood from forest was taken and used as fuel between 1935-1965. Between 1966 and 1980, fire wood and agricultural waste were used as fuel. Kerosene was another type of fuel that was used as fuel, apart from agricultural wastes, between the years 1981-1997.

Utensils

All kinds of utensils made out of mud, were used between the years 1935-1965. Mud pots, aluminium pots and brass utensils were used during 1966-1980. Stainless steel replaced the use of marks and it is in use till to day along with mud pots and aluminium utensils.

Entertainment

Entertainment is an important social activity in any community living. Hunting was the prime form of entertainment for the people of Palamathi Hills from 1935–1980. Drama became a part of entertainment between 1966 and 1980. Cinema and television replaced these entertainments between 1981-1987.

INFRASTRUCTURE

Public utilities and resource like water supply, sewage disposal, roads, highway, parks, electrical lines, communication system, drainage, buses and other transportation facilities etc constitute the main infrastructure requirements. The responsibility of providing these usually rests with the public sector.

Roads

There are two approaches to the Palamathi Hills; one road connects the hamlets namely Palamathi, Krishnapuram, Chetteri and Arasankulam.While the other road is accessible to the Chenganatham hamlet. The total length of the former tar road in Palamathi village is 9 km. While, the mud road is 1 km long. The hill village also has concrete roads at some public places like the temple and in Chetteri Indira Memorial Street totaling to a length of 488.33 meters. The total length of the tar road is 4.9 kms. There are eight hairpin bends on the Palamathi Hill road that begins at the foot hill and ends at the Palamathi Hills.

Transport

Public buses are available that ply from the hill village to the town and to the neighbouring places. All buses ply from Vellore Bus stand. One bus route starts from, Vellore bus stand and reaches Thimiri covering a distance of 25 Kms.Another bus route starts from Vellore and reaches Chenganatham covering about 10 kms.The main bus stand is at Vellore. The buses ply between the Vellore Bus stand and the neighbouring places. Their nearest railway station is the Katpadi Railway station. It is nearly 16km from Palamathi hill village. The railway lines are connected with a good network of roads. The people own mopeds, cars, bicycle, autos etc.for their own transportation.

Water Supply System

Apart from wells and bore wells, public water supply is received in some areas of Palamathi.

Electricity Supply

Electrification of the hill village has also been done. It has 43 streetlights.

Communication System

The hill village has 2 public telephone booths, one at Chenganatham and another at Palamathi. There is no post office. A few families have telephones that cater to their communication need.

Other Facilities

There are 4 nutritious noon meal centers, 5 panchayat buildings, 2 child care centers, 1 community hall, 2 public television halls.

SCHOOL

There is a School each in the following hamlets viz., Palamathi, Chettari, Krishnapuram and Chenganatham.The hill village has two PDS Center. A Veterinary hospital is located at Chettari.

DEVELOPMENTAL ACTIVITIES OF PALAMATHI HILL VILLAGE, 1960-2000.

- In 1960, the village panchayat in Palamathi hill village was started by the Govt.of Tamil Nadu.
- Between 1962 and 1964, beginners primary school was started in the Chenganatham hamlet.
- An orientation training in Rural Development was given to the panchayat head at the orientation study center. Bhavani Sagar, Coimbatore between the period 26-8-63 to 14 -9-63. Electricity connection was given to Palamathi and Chenganatham.
- Between 1968 and 1978, 3 ½ lakhs was spent to lay roads in the Vellore, Kanniyambadi and Timiri Panchayat Union.
- In 1970 the Chettari Elementary School was started.
- On 15-03-1994 transportation between Vellore –Timiri was started.
- In 1980, Elementary School in Krishnapuram was started.
- Between 1982-84 tar road was laid for Chenganatham hamlet.
- In 1995, Elementary school was started in the Palamathi hamlet.
- In 1999 buses started to ply to Chenganatham hamlet.
- On 18-01-2000 Rural Development, Development allotted 5 lakhs for Palamathi hills in Vellore Panchayat Union.

Summary table of all activities and financial allocation since 1996-1997 till 2000-2001 placed in table 10.

EXPENDITURE ON DEVELOPMENT ACTIVITIES

1. Jawahar Rozgar Yojana

   Financial year 1997 to 2001.Total allocation was 1,80,282.

Table 10
Palamathi Panchayat
Summary Table of all Activities and Financial Allocation Since 1996-1997 Till 2000-2001.

Sl. No	Name of Scheme and Implementing Agency	1996-1997		1997-1998		1998-1999		1999-2000		2000-2001		Total of four years		Total Works	
		No of Works	Amount	No of Works	Amount	No of Works	Amount	No of Works	Amount	No of Works	Amount	No of Works	Amount	No of Works	Amount
1.	Jawahar Rozar Yojana	-	-	1	29135	2	91203	1	29144	1	30800	-	-	5	180282
2.	Indian Memorial Housing Scheme	-	-	-	-	1	640000	-	-	1	160000		-	2	800000
3.	10th Finance Commission	2	30780	1	8516	2	42706	1	33000	-	-	-	-	6	114002
4.	State Financial Commission	-	-	1	33773	1	200000	-	-	-	-	-	-	2	133773
5.	Employment guarantee scheme	-	-	1	132000	4	829000	-	-	-	-	-	-	5	961000
6.	Constituency Development Fund through MP	-	-	-	-	1	229000	-	-	-	-	-	-	1	229000
7.	Constituency Development fund through MLA	-	-	-	-	1	50000	-	-	-	-	-	-	1	50000
8.	Underdeveloped Panchayat Scheme	-	-	1	30000	5	145000	-	-	-	-	-	-	6	175000
9.	Equalization and Motivation subsidy finance and establishment of Tourism Development cener	-	-	-	-	1	199800	2	500000	-	-	-	-	3	699800

Sl. No	Name of Scheme and Implementing Agency	1996-1997		1997-1998		1998-1999		1999-2000		2000-2001		Total of four years		Total Works	
		No of Works	Amount	No of Works	Amount	No of Works	Amount	No of Works	Amount	No of Works	Amount	No of Works	Amount	No of Works	Amount
10.	Parliamentary Constituency Development Fund	-	-	-	-	-	-	2	750000	-	-	-	-	2	750000
11.	Namaku Namay Thitam	-	-	-	-	-	-	5	646000	-	-	-	-	5	646000
12.	High ways Department	-	-	-	-	-	-	2	1075000	-	-	-	-	2	1075000
13.	Central Govt. Rajiv Gandhi Drinking water Schemes	-	-	-	-	-	-	11	570000	-	-	-	-	11	570000
14.	Drought Prone Area Programme (DPAP)	16	808412	8	466718	4	194296	1	100000	-	-	-	-	29	1569426
15.	Tamil Nadu drinking water and drainage Works	-	-	-	-	-	-	1	559000	3	2204000	-	-	4	2763000
16.	Guaranteed Employment Scheme	-	-	1	50000	1	75000	1	200000	-	-	-	-	3	325000
17.	Tamil Nadu Forest Development Scheme:														
	(a) Vellore Social Forestry Scheme	-	-	11	623851	11	256748	6	115550	-	-	4	2244940	32	3241089
	(b) Vellore Social Forestry Scheme	-	-			17	1407391	6	440609	1	70000	4	1196645	28	3114645
	Total	18	839192	25	1373993	51	4259144	28	4448303	17	034800	8	3441585	147	17397017

Source: Palamathi Hill Panchayat Office Records.

Activities: Building of landslide prevention wall, roads, TV community rooms, cement roads, SC Colony.

2. Indira Memorial housing Scheme

   Financial year 1998 to 2001 = Total allocation was 8,00,000

   Activities: 25 House constructions for SC People.

3. 10th Finance commission , subsidy for works

   Financial year 1996 to 2000 = Total allocation was 1,14,002.

   Activities: Streetlights, bore wells, widening of roads, cement roads etc.

4. State Financial Commission, subsidy for works.

   Financial year 1997 to 1999 = Total allocation was I,33,777.

5. Employment guarantee scheme (Vellore panchayat Union)

   Financial year 1997 to 1999 = Total allocation was 9,61,000

   Activities: Fair price shop building, tar roads, bus stop.

6. Constituency Development Fund through. MP.

   Financial year 1998 to 1999 =Total allocation was 2,29,000.

   Activities: Primary school building construction.

7. Constituency Development Fund through MLA.

   Financial year 1998 to 1999 = Total allocation was 50,000

   Activities: Cement roads.

8. Under developed Panchayat Scheme

   Financial year 1997 to 1999 =Total allocation was 1,75,000

   Activities: Digging bore well, electrical connection and writing works.

9. Equalization and Motivation subsidy finance and establishment of Tourism Development Center.

   Financial year 1998 to 2000 = Total allocation was 6,99,800

   Activities: repair works of temple, rest house, developing aesthetic beauty at Murugan Temple.

10. Parliamentary Constituency Development Fund

    Total allocation was 7,50,000.

Activities: Compound wall, tar roads etc.

11. Namaku Namay Thitham (25% were contributed by the villagers)

    Financial year 1999to 2000 = Total allocation was 6,46,000.

    Activities: Compound wall, thoroughfare, leveling of ground, ground water tank, bore well and fixing of motor.

12. High ways Department:

    Total allocation was 10,75,000.

    Activities: Highway Maintenance and renovation.

13. Central Govt. Rajiv Gandhi Drinking Water Schemes (10% contributed by the people)

    Total allocation was 5,70,000

    Activities: Overhead tanks, Nutritious noon meal center, hand pumps.

14. Drought Prone Area Programme (DPAP)

    Financial year 1996 to 2000 = Total allocation was 15,69,426
    Activities: Compound wall for meal center, drainage, compound wall for primary school, cleaning of ponds and widening them, building of check dams, ploughs for farmers, implements for leveling ground given to farmers, seed and fertilizers for farmers, distribution of saplings such as pongamia, neem, cotton, babul etc to farmers, and for home kitchen gardens etc.

15. Tamilnadu drinking water and drainage works

    Financial year 1999 to 2001 = Total allocation was 27,63,000

    Activities: Overhead tanks, and distribution of pipe connection in 4 different hamlets.

16. Guaranteed Employment Scheme (Agricultural Department)

    Financial year 1997to 2000 = Total allocation was 3,25,000
    Activities: Compound wall, cleaning and widening of ponds and temple ponds.

TAMILNADU FOREST DEVELOPMENT SCHEME

(a) Vellore social Forestry Scheme

Financial year 1997 to 2000 = Total allocation 32,41,089

Activities: Overhead tanks, roadside trees, white washing school compound wall advertisement boards, awareness campus about forests, loans for sewing machine, iron box, hybrid cows, provision stores, electrical instruments, mini restaurant, vegetable shops etc, free smokeless Chula, free chemical sprayer, planting of tree saplings in leeward side of the hill etc.

(b) Tamil Nadu Forest Development Scheme

Financial year 1998to 2001 = Total allocation was 31,14,645

Activities: Overhead tanks, white washing school compound wall, loan for basket weaving, tailoring training, loan for purchase of milch cow, seedling multiplication training, free mango sapling distribution, free smokeless Chula, planting of tree saplings (afforestation) in the down slope, up slope, central slope and in water logged areas.

PLACES OF WORSHIP

For most Indians, religion is a way of life. Indian homes usually have a separate room or niche, which holds a sacred object or idol to which the family pays daily obeisance. Many invasions resulted in the diversity of religions in the country. However, Hinduism is predominant. In the social network, temples form an integral part in the life of Hindu devotees. Hinduism, a polytheistic religion, has many Gods and their incarnations. The people of Palamathi are mainly Hindus and they worship many deities.

Deities

There are three temples at Palamathi.They are:

- The Ganapathy temple at the foot hills , built in 1970.
- The Anjeneya Temple at the peak of the hills, built in 1929.
- The Murugan temple located 1 km away from the former temple, built in 1970.

People worship Anjeneyar and Murugan. People who worship Anjeneyar are called Vaishanavites and the latter are called Dakshanamurthyites.

Festivals

The most important festivals celebrated by the people here are:

- The Saral Vilzha–celebrated during June when the monsoon sets in.
- The Pongal Festival– celebrated during January when food crops are harvested from the field.
- Vinayaga Chathurthi during September.

TOURISM

"Tourism is the sum of the phenomenon and relationship arising from travel and stay of non-residents, in so far as they do not lead to permanent residence and are not connected with any earning activity".[1]

Since Palamathi is a hill village it has some unique attractions of its own that can be enhanced in order to develop it as a tourist spot. *"Tourism is a smokeless industry"*. that earns revenue for the places where tourism activity is done. This hill village was also used by cinematographers for film shooting.

Tourist Spots at Palamathi

The Palamathi hills have many tourist attractions in order to be developed as a tourist place. It has a lotus pond at the fourth hairpin bend. It is a very beautiful sight. The Kuzhandhai Velayudhapani temple, a banyan tree growing on a rock, The Veera Anjanayar temple built in 1929 by digging a cave in the rock, an old tank dug in 1932, Matheankulam waterfalls in chettari, the natural scenic beauty at Karamalai, Kotaimalai and Perungamalai, the teak forest and land scape of Chenganatham are some of the tourist spots of this hill village.

Tourism Prospects in Palamathi Hill

Since Palamathi hill village is a potential site for tourism development, the Government intends to undertake the following activities.

- Building of rest house.
- Binocular tower .
- Boating at Mathankulam, Chettari hamlet.
- Establishment of a mini zoo and children's park.

NOTE

1. Priyan C. Oomen,(1989) "Global's Tourism Directory of India" Global Communication Pvt. Ltd, Trivandrum, p. 1.

4

DESIGN OF THE STUDY

QUANTITATIVE TOOLS

Correlation Method

For finding the relationship between the income and expenditure of the study area, correlation coefficient of the following form was used.

$$r = \frac{\Sigma xy}{\sqrt{\Sigma x^2 x \Sigma y^2}}$$

Where,

r = correlation

Sxy = sum of xy value

Sx^2 = sum of x^2 value

Sy^2 = sum of y^2 value

Correlation Matrix

Correlation coefficients were calculated between variables x_1 and x_2, x_3, x_1 and x_4 x_1 and x_5, x_1 and x_6. Also between x_2 and x_3, x_2 and x_4, x_2 and x_5, x_2 and x_6 and so on. Where,

x_1 = Marketable Surplus

x_2 = Net Area

x_3 = Out put

x_4 = Family size

x_5 = Consumption
x_6 = Expenditure

Regression Analysis

Regression model was used to determine whether or not a relationship exists between two variables, to describe the nature of relationship and to assess the relative importance of the various predictor variables. Here, marketable surplus is treated as dependent variable. Net area, output, family size and price are treated as independent variables.

Regression model

$$Y = \beta_0 + \beta_1 X_1 + \beta_2 X_2 + \beta_3 X_3 + \beta_4 X_4 + E$$

Where,

Y = Marketable Surplus
b = Beta
X_1 = Net Area
X_2 = Out put
X_3 = Family size
X_4 = Price of paddy
E = Random Error

ELASTICITY OF MARKETED SURPLUS WITH RESPECT TO NET AREA

Elasticity of Demand

The concept of elasticity of demand refers to the degree of responsiveness of quantity demanded of a good to a change in its price, income or prices of related goods.

Formula

$$\text{Elasticity} = \frac{\%\text{ change in demanded}}{\%\text{ change in Price}}$$

$$= \frac{\Delta q}{\Delta p} \times \frac{p}{q}$$

= q stands for quantity.
= p stands for price.
= D stands for infinitesimal change.

MEASUREMENT OF TREND IN THE MIGRATION OF THE RESPONDENTS

Formula

$$Y = a + bx$$

Where,

Y = The estimated values of the trend

X = The deviation in some convenient time periods

'a' and 'b'are the constant 'a' (or) the parameters

'a' refers to the constant 'a' y-intercept (i.e.) the difference between the point of the origin (o), and the point where the trend line touches the y-axis.

'b' refers to the constant 'b' the line which indicates the change in y for each unit change in x.

T-TEST

Under t-test, independent sample test was conducted to study the level of variances of illiterates and literates, on the dependent variable income.

Formula

$$t = \frac{r}{\sqrt{1-r^2}} \times \sqrt{n-2}$$

The t- test value is compared to critical value at n – 2 degrees of freedom. The calculated t-value is less than the table at n – 2 degrees of freedom. The calculated t-value is less than the table at n-2 degrees of freedom at 5 per cent level of significance, then it is said that the sample could have come from the population (literacy). And if he calculated value 't' is more than the table value, it is said that there is a significant difference between the sample and population data.

5

ANALYSIS AND INTERPRETATION

INTRODUCTION

The present study is intended to make a microscopic analysis of the socio-economic condition of the inhabitants of Palamathi Hills in Tamil Nadu. The objectives and hypothesis were presented in the first chapter. The important concepts, used in the study were reviewed and presented in the second chapter. The description of the Palamathi hill village was presented in the third chapter. The research design forms a part of the fourth chapter.

The present chapter attempts to make an in depth economic analysis of the primary data that was collected from the entire population. It is later classified, tabulated and examined.

For the purpose of analysis, 366 sample households in Palamathi hill village were classified according to their annual income during the year 2001–2002. The households of the study area were classified into five income groups. The following classification of households is adopted for the entire study.

ORIGIN AND SETTLEMENT

Palamathi, a virgin hillock, has attracted people from in and around Vellore and from various parts of Andhra Pradesh and Karnataka states. The place of birth of migrants and the number of migrants from each place are presented in (Fig 1).

Table 1
Classification of respondents according to their Annual Income

S. No	*Income range (Per annum)*	*Annual Income*	*Per cent (%)*
1.	Below 12,000	19,84,500.00	36.33
2.	12,001 – 24,000	8,37,500.00	15.33
3.	24,001 – 36,000	12,66,150.00	23.18
4.	36,001 – 48,000	9,25,450.20	16.94
5.	48,001 – 64,000	4,48,500.00	8.22
	Total	54,62,100.20	100.00

Source: Primary data.

Fig. 1: Origin of Migration

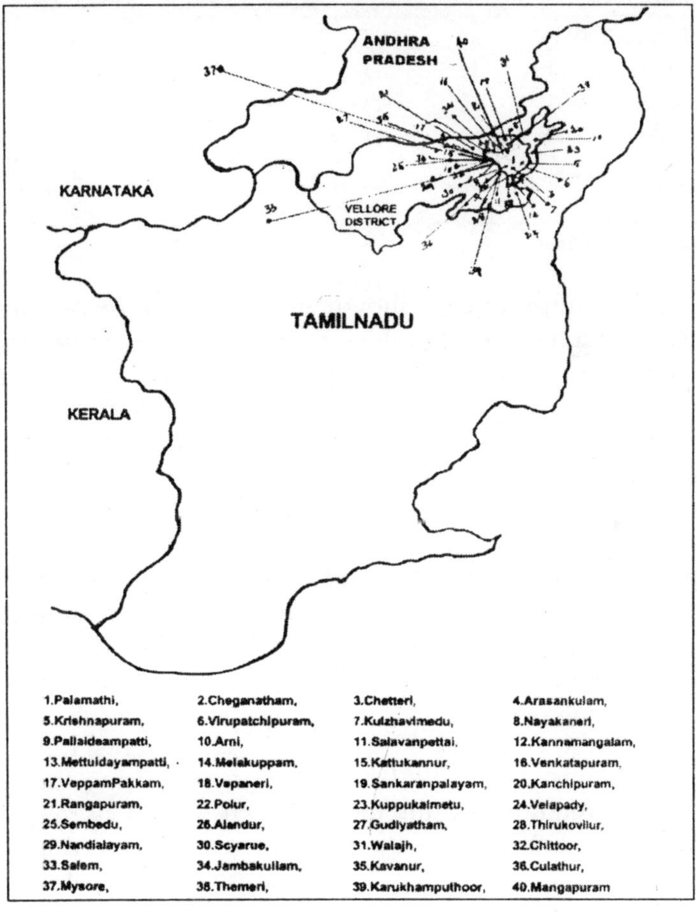

Persons Migrated

Migration to Palamathi hills had started as early as 1886. The kinship system often determines who in the family will migrate (Janet Rodenberg, 1993). The grandparents of the present generation have migrated first. Who migrated first in the family? The answers given by the respondents were classified and presented in table 2 below.

Table 2
Persons Migrated

S. No.	*Income range (Per annum)*	*Self*	*Father*	*Grand-father*	*Grand-mother*	*Grand-parents*	*Total*
1.	Below 12,000	42	48	5	6	88	189
2.	12,001 – 24,000	12	11	2	3	39	67
3.	24,001 – 36,000	9	23	3	3	31	69
4.	36,001 – 48,000	4	11	3	-	10	28
5.	48,001 – 64,000	4	3	1	-	5	13
	Total	71	96	14	12	173	366

Source: Primary data.

Among migrants, as shown in table 3, 71 respondents (19.39%) migrated by themselves. In 96 households, father alone migrated first followed by other members of the family. Grandfather migrated first in the households (3.82%). Grandmothers had migrated in 12 households (3.27%). Grandparents migrated in 173 households (47.26%).

Year of Migration

The year of migration of the respondents, as reported by the respondents, is presented in table 3. It could be seen that out of 366 households, highest number of respondents, 202 (55.19%) had migrated before the year 1950. the subsequent years had seen fall in migration.

During the year 1951-60, there were 49 migrants, followed by 37 migrants during 1961-70, 44 migrants during the year 1971-80, 20 migrants during the year 1981-90 and 14 migrants during the year1991-2000. As years progressed the migrants declined. It is in conformity with Ricardo's theory of rent in which people will occupy less fertile land as population increases. The unabated migration has overpopulated the Palamathi hills and it has slowed down the pace of migration from 1950–2000. The tend in migration between 1950–2000 was calculated and presented in table 3.

Table 3
Year of Migration by the Respondents

S. No.	*Income range (Per annum)*	*Before 1950*	*1951-1960*	*1961-1970*	*1971-1980*	*1981-1990*	*1991-2000*	*Total*
1.	Below 12,000	107	31	19	19	8	5	189
2.	12,001 – 24,000	45	3	2	5	5	7	67
3.	24,001 – 36,000	33	9	13	9	3	2	69
4.	36,001 – 48,000	13	5	1	7	2	-	28
5.	48,001 – 64,000	4	1	2	4	2	-	13
	Total	202	49	37	44	20	14	366

Source: Primary data.

Measurement of Trend Line in the Migration of the respondents

The commonly used methods for the study and measurement of the trend are free hand and graphic method, semi average method, moving average methods and least squares method. In this study, graphic method is used. This method is very simple and flexible in estimating trend. The procedure to obtain straight line trend is to plot the given time series data on graph and draw a straight line on the data

Table 4
Trend in the Migration of Respondents in Palamathi Hills

S. No	*Year*	*Y Migration of respondents*	*X*	*X^2*	*XY*	*Yc (Trend value)*
1.	Before 1950	202	0	0	0	61.0
2.	1951-1960	49	1	1	49	68.36
3.	1961-1970	37	2	4	74	75.72
4.	1971-1980	44	3	9	132	83.08
5.	1981-1990	20	4	16	80	90.44
	1991-2000	14	5	25	70	97.80
	N=6	$\Sigma Y=366$	$\Sigma X=15$	$\Sigma X^2 = 55$	$\Sigma XY= 405$	476.40

The equation of the straight line trend is, Y = a+bx

$$a = \frac{\Sigma Y}{n}, \qquad b = \frac{\Sigma XY}{\Sigma X^2}$$

$\Sigma Y = 366$

$N = 6$

$\Sigma Y = 15$

$\Sigma XY = 405$

$$a = \frac{\Sigma Y}{n},$$

$$a = \frac{366}{6} = 61 \qquad a = 61$$

$$b = \frac{\Sigma Y}{\Sigma X^2}$$

$$b = \frac{405}{55} = 7.36$$

$b = 7.36$

The following fig. 2 illustrates the trend in the migration of respondents in Palamathi Hills from the year 1950 onwards.

Fig. 2: Trend in the Migration of Respondents

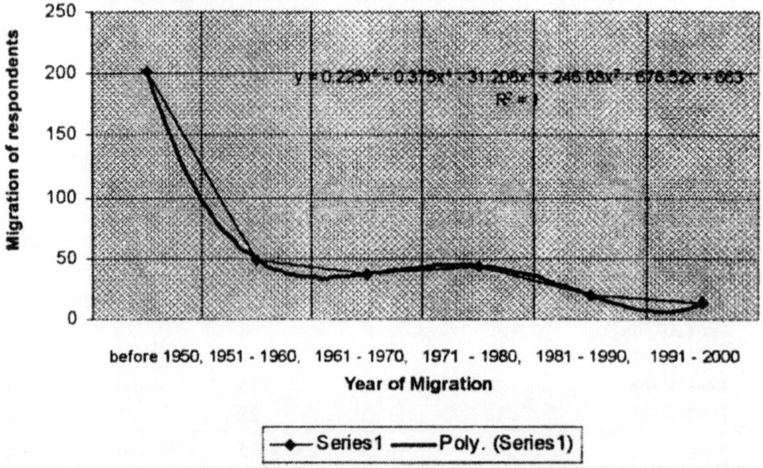

The trend line shows a downward slope, expressing fall in the migration of the people to the Palamathi Hills.

Reasons for Migration

Both pull and push factors have operated in the case of migration to Palamathi hills. The push factors are the fertile land of Palamathi hill, sparsely populated area, which is free from communal clash and a peaceful atmosphere. On the contrary, the places from where the people had migrated were overcrowded with less land and more people. Lack of employment opportunities, communal clashes and tensions had pushed them to Palamathi hills. As reported in table 5, majority of the migrants (51.63 per cent) had come to Palamathi in search of job and land. 159 household (43.44 per cent) had faced acute shortage in their place of origin, therefore they preferred to migrate to Palamathi. People who faced social problems and social tensions had migrated to Palamathi.

Table 5
Reasons for Migration

S. No.	*Income range (Per annum)*	*Lack of land*	*Lack of employ-ment*	*Social problems*	*Other reasons*	*Total*
1.	Below 12,000	71	110	1	7	189
2.	12,001 – 24,000	31	31	2	3	67
3.	24,001 – 36,000	33	32	1		69
4.	36,001 – 48,000	15	12	-	1	28
5.	48,001 – 64,000	9	4	-	-	13
	Total	159 (43.44)	189 (51.63)	4 (1.09)	14 (3.82)	366 (100)

Note: Figures in parenthesis indicates percentage to the total distance between place of Migration and Palamathi.

Distance from the Place of Migration

The migrants of Palamathi hills had travelled from near and far off places. As shown in Table 6, 46 respondents (12.56 per cent) had travelled one kilometer to reach Palamathi. 52 respondents (14.20) had travelled 2 kilometers 98 respondents (26.77 per cent) had travelled 3 kilometers, 10 (2.73 per cent) of respondents had travelled 10 kilometers, 35 respondents travelled 23 kilometers, 54 respondents (14.75 per cent) had travelled 20 kilometers, 45 respondents (12.29 per cent) had travelled 25 kilometers and 13 respondents had traveled beyond 25 kilometers. The number of persons and the distance travelled did not show any uniformity as indicated in Table 6.

Table 6
Distance from the place of Migration

S. No.	*Income range in Rs. (Per annum)*	*Distance in Kilometers (Km)*									*Total*
		1	*2*	*3*	*5*	*10*	*15*	*20*	*25*	*³ 25*	
1.	Below 12,000	19	27	52	2	3	23	31	25	7	189
2.	12,001 – 24,000	6	12	12	2	3	7	13	9	3	67
3.	24,001 – 36,000	10	11	22	3	3	3	8	6	3	69
4.	36,001 – 48,000	7	2	11	2	3	-	-	3	-	28
5.	48,001 – 64,000	4	-	1	1	1	2	2	2	-	
	Total	46 (12.56)	52 (14.20)	98 (26.77)	10 (2.73)	13 (3.55)	35 (9.56)	54 (14.75)	45 (12.29)	13 (3.55)	366 (100)

Note: Figures in parenthesis indicate percentage to the total.

The distance of migration from 1Km up to 3 Km, the number of people migrated had increased. But the 4th Kilometer witnessed a steep fall in migration. Subsequently, the number of people migrated increased with distance. The people, who faced problems at the plains, did not consider distance as a burden. Necessity compels a person to move out and forces him to search a better habitat. The people of Palamathi hills have opted to adopt Palamathi as their habitat. The movement of the people to Palamathi hills has approved the hypothesis, that distance never desisted the people from travelling to Palamathi.

Occupation of the Grand-Parents

A study on the occupation of the grand parents would enable to find out the change of occupations.

The occupation of the grandparents, as shown in Fig. 3, reveals that majority of them were either engaged in agriculture or worked as agricultural coolies. The remaining 10 per cent of the grand parents had worked as masons, dhobi, quarry workers, and engaged in business, goat rearing, carpentry and basket making.

Fig. 3: Occupation of the Grandparents

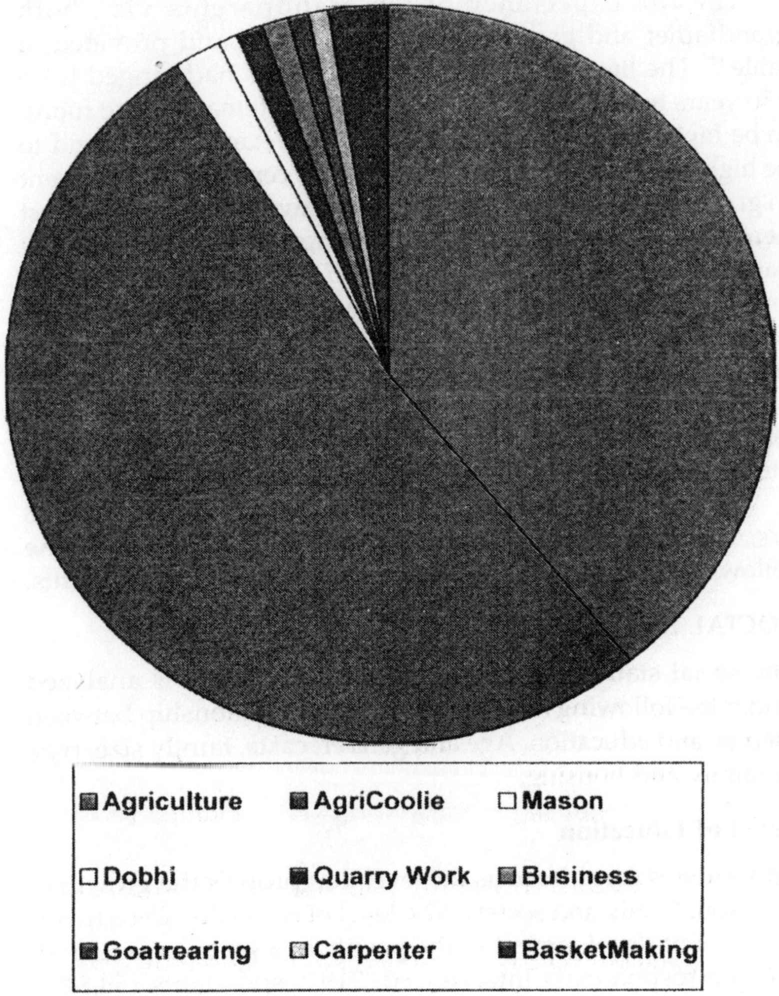

Life Expectancy of Grandparents

The life expectancy or expectation of life at a given age is the average number of years which a person of the age may expect to live according to the mortality pattern prevalent in that country. Demographers consider it as one of the best indicators of a country's level of development and of the overall health status of its population.[1]

The life expectancy of the grandparents viz., both grandfather and grandmother were studied and provided in table 7. The life expectancy of grandparents had ranged from <50 years to > 70 years. The expectancy of females were found to be higher than the males. The life expectancy was found to be high above 70 yrs to the tune of 28 per cent and 29.6 per cent in grandfather and grandmother respectively. The next highest percentage was recorded in the age range of 61-70 yrs and they gave a value of 15.44 per cent and 15.57 per cent in grandfathers and grandmothers respectively. However, the life expectancy was very high in the case of females to the tune of 15.44 per cent above 70 yrs.

It is worth mentioning that, in males, the life expectancy decreased with increase in income. While in the females, the life expectancy did not have much effect on income level.

The average life expectancy of males were found to be 66.88 yrs, while in the females, it was found to be 69.6 yrs. The following table 7 indicates the life expectancy of grandparents.

SOCIAL STATUS

The social status of the people of Palamathi hill is analyzed under the following headings: education, relationship between income and education. Age and gender, caste, family size, type of family and housing.

Level of Education

Education is considered as the level that propels the growth of a person, family and society. The level of education determines the level of development of the people in a given area. Out of the 366 respondents interviewed, 219 respondents (59.84%) were illiterates. The distribution of illiterates among various income group shows that more than 50% of the illiterates belong to the first group (those who have annual income less than Rs.12,000). The remaining 44 per cent of the illiterates are

Table 7
Life expectancy of Grandparents

S. No.	Income group (Rupees/annum)	Below 50 yrs		51 – 60 yrs		61 – 70 yrs		Above 70 yrs.		No response		Total
		Male	Female	Male	Female	Male	Female	Male	Female	Male	Female	
1.	Below 12,000	7	2	13	7	64	62	104	113	1	5	378
2.	12,001 – 24,000	1	1	5	4	17	15	42	45	2	2	134
3.	24,001 – 36,000	0	0	7	2	23	25	35	39	4	3	138
4.	36,000 – 48,000	1	0	4	3	7	9	15	14	1	2	56
5.	48,001 – 64,000	0	1	0	0	2	3	9	6	2	3	26
	Total	9 (1.23)	4 (0.55)	29 (3.96)	16 (2.19)	113 (15.44)	114 (15.57)	205 (28.00)	217 (29.64)	10 (1.37)	15 (2.05)	732 (100)

Note: Figures in parenthesis indicate percentage to the total

distributed among the other four income groups. The distribution of illiterates among the various income group shows concentration of illiteracy among low income group.

The 147 literate respondents are distributed among different levels of education. From the study it was found that 68 respondents (18.58%) had studied up to primary school, 66 respondents (18.03%) had studied up to middle school, five respondents (1.37%) had studied up to high school, three respondents (0.18%) had studied up to higher secondary school, and five respondents (1.37% had done higher education. Fig. 4 illustrates the level of education of the respondents.

Fig. 4: Level of Education of the Respondents

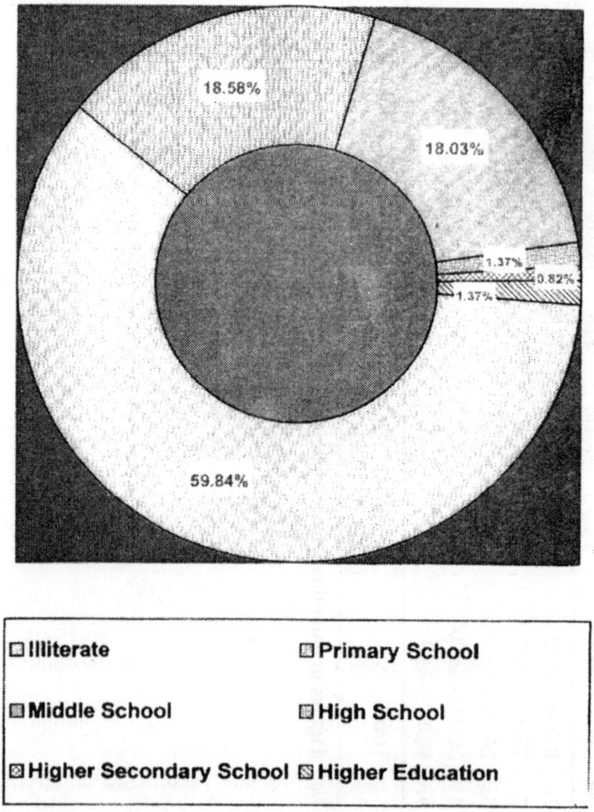

t-Test on Income and Education

Under t-test, independent sample test was conducted to study the level of variances of illiterates, on the dependent variable, income. The result of t-test is given below.

Table 8
Group statistics

Educational status of the person	*Number*	*Mean*	*Std Deviation*	*Std. Error Mean*
Illiterate	217	19,309.14	11,635.47	789.87
Literate	150	19,358.32	12,309.78	1,005.09

The test yields a probability of .68. Because this probability is greater than .05, it concludes that the t-test statistics is based on equal variances. Next, the t-test for differences in the two means were considered. Since the equal variance method was adopted, the results were read from the first line of the t-test's (Labeled "Equal variance assumed").

The result is, at value of -.04, with 365 degrees of freedom and a probability of .97. Since this is greater than .05, it can be concluded that illiterates and literates had similar mean income.

It was also observed from the results that the mean difference between the two groups was –49.18. Although this was the observed difference, the 95% confidence interval of the difference in the means is somewhere between –2,537.20 and 2,466.64.

Age and Gender wise Classification of Respondents

There were 323 male headed families and 43 female headed families in Palamathi hills while conducting the survey.

The gender of respondents among various age group showed that 24 males (6.56 %) belonged to 31–40 yrs age group, 199 (29.78%) belonged to the age group of 41–50 yrs, while 66 (18.03 per cent) respondents belonged to 51–60 age group. Majority of the male respondent belonged to post adult group. Otherwise they belonged to the ageing population.

The distribution of female respondents among various age group shows that the female respondents belonged to 31–40

Table 9
Independent Sample Test

		Levene's test of equality of variance		*t- Test for equality of means*						
		F	*Sig.*	*t*	*df*	*Sig (2-tailed)*	*Mean difference*	*Std. Error Difference*	*95% confidence interval of the difference*	
									lower	*upper*
Income	Equal variances assumed	.173	.68	-.04	365	.97	-49.18	1,265.21	-2,537.20	2,438.85
	Equal variances not assumed	-	-	-.04	308.662	.97	-49.18	1,278.32	-2564.50	2,466.14

Table 10
Age and Gender wise Classification of the Head of the Family

S. No.	*Income group*	*20 – 30*		*31 – 40*		*41 – 50*		*51 – 60*		*Above 60*		*Total*	
		Male	*Female*	*Male*	*Female*	*Male*	*Female*	*Male*	*Female*	*Male*	*Female*	*Male*	*Female*
1.	Below 12,000	8	0	24	1	58	9	32	14	37	6	159	30
2.	12,001 – 24,000	6	0	18	0	19	0	12	3	7	2	62	5
3.	24,001 – 36,000	6	0	10	0	23	0	13	2	12	3	64	5
4.	36,000 – 48,000	4	0	4	0	6	1	5	1	7	0	26	2
5.	48,001 – 64,000	-	0	1	0	3	0	4	0	4	1	12	1
	Total	24 (6.56)	0	57 (15.51)	1 (0.27)	119 (29.78)	10 (2.73)	66 (18.03)	20 (5.46)	67 (18.30)	12 (3..28)	323 (88..25)	43 (11.75)

Note: figures in parenthesis are percentage to total

yrs age group, 10 respondents belonged to 41–50 age group, 20 respondents belonged to above 60 yrs. In age the female respondents were not found to be different from their male counterparts and they too belonged to the ageing population of Palamathi hill. It is explicitly mentioned in table 10.

Caste-wise Classification

India is the largest democratic and populous nation in the world and is still ravaged by the system of caste in it's social structure. In the Palamathi village only 3 castes were identified viz., Schedule caste, Most Backward Caste and Backward Caste. The study revealed that 60.11 per cent of the people belonged to the Most Backward Caste, while 27.59% and 12.30 per cent of the people belonged to the Backward Caste and Scheduled Caste respectively. It was also found in all the three castes, the highest per cent of the population were in the income range of Rs. <12,000/- year. The number of people decreased in all the three castes with increasing income group. This is depicted in Fig. 5. Literature reveals that majority of the studies on hill stations were inhabited by tribes of homogenous type.

Size of the Family

It is generally believed that the size of the family determines the prosperity of the family. Poor families are large in size and rich families are small in size.

The details on the size of the family collected from the respondents are presented in Table 11 As shown in the table, the number of families had increased with size up to five members after which it declined.

The average size of the family was also calculated income wise and presented in table 15 the total population of all the households was enumerated as 2172. and the average size of all the households was calculated as 5.93. But the income wise average size of families gave a different picture. The lowest income group had the smallest average size of 4.79. The average family size of the second income group was calculated as 7.68, followed by 6.10 in the third group, 6.35 in the fourth income group and 11.64 in the last income group. This was against the

Fig. 5: Caste Wise Classification

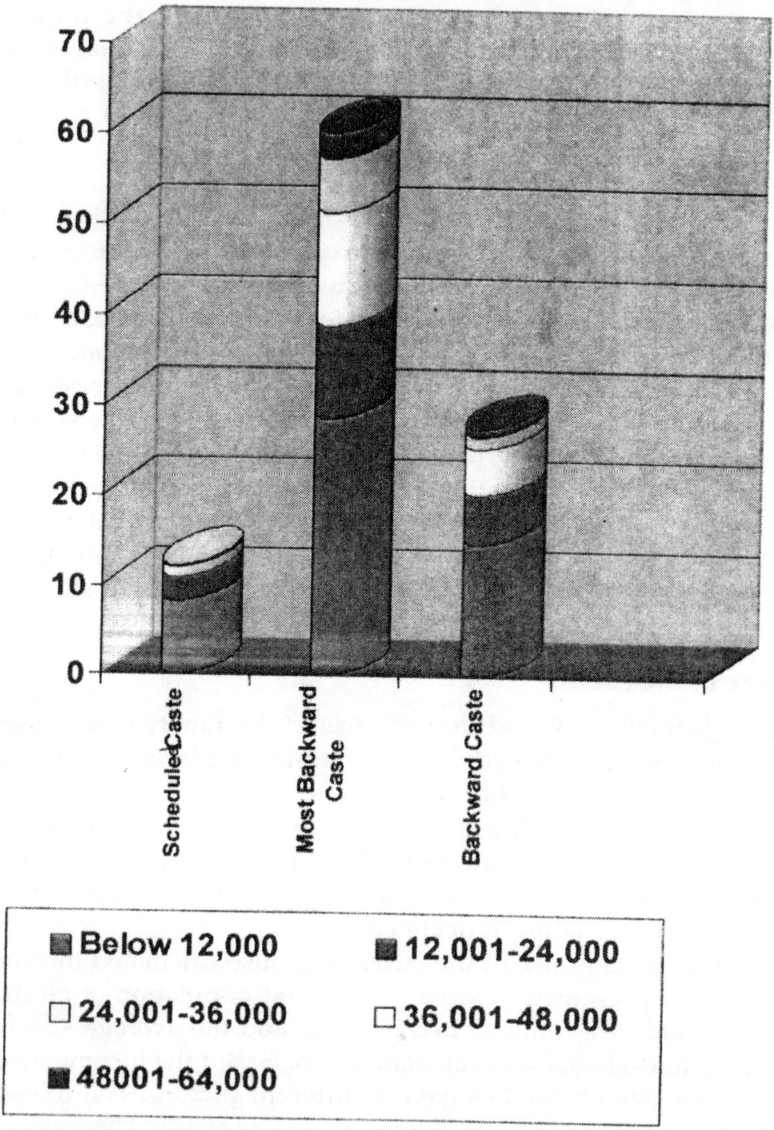

widely held notion among the people of Palamathi that the average size of families increased with income. Therefore there is an urgent need for bringing down the size of families in this study area. This can be done through proper education in the hill.

Table 11
Family size

S. No	*Income group*	*Number of members in the family* 1	2	3	4	5	6	7	8	9	10	>10	*Total Popu- lation*	*Ave- rage size*
1.	Below 12,000	7	22	24	49	41	23	5	8	2	1	7	907	4.79
2.	12,001 – 24,000	1	7	8	16	13	9	8	2	1	1	1	515	7.68
3.	24,001 – 36,000	0	3	10	13	23	4	6	4	2	2	2	421	6.10
4.	36,000 – 48,000	0	0	4	3	1	4	2	0	1	1	2	178	6.35
5.	48,001 – 64,000	0	0	1	2	2	2	1	0	1	1	3	151	11.64
	Total	8	32	47	83	90	42	22	14	7	6	15	2172	5.93

Type of Family

Besides size, type also is an important indicator of the status of the family. The joint families and the extended families are considered as traditional, where as nuclear families are considered as modern. In setting up families, the people in Palamathi gave importance to modern family. Therefore as shown in table 12 there were 292 families (79.29%) that were found to have a nuclear setup. Among the remaining families, there were 43 (11.74%) joint families and 31 (8.46%) extended families.

Table 12
Type of Family

S. No.	*Income group (Rupees/annum)*	*Joint*	*Extended*	*Nuclear*	*Total*
1.	Below 12,000	18	11	160	189
2.	12,001 – 24,000	4	9	54	67
3.	24,001 – 36,000	11	6	52	69
4.	36,000 – 48,000	4	3	21	28
5.	48,001 – 64,000	6	2	5	13
	Total	43 (11.74)	31 (8.46)	292 (79.79)	366 (100)

Note: Figures in parenthesis are percentage to total.

Nature of House

The nature of house owned and occupied by the people were based on their economic status and the houses were classified as Kutcha, Thatched roof, Tiled roof, Reinforced cement concrete (R.C.C) roof and Group houses. Group houses are houses built by the Government for the benefit of the weaker section. 136 (37.15%) had owned R.C.C roof houses, followed by 76 (20.77%) who owned kutcha houses, 73 (19.55%) owned thatched houses and 52 (14.20%) owned tiled roof house. There were 29 group houses, which was restricted to the first three income groups viz., from < Rs.12,000 to Rs. 36,000. It was amazing to note that RCC roof houses were also owned by the lower income group. This was because the respondents had availed liberal bank loan facility. It also shows their eagerness to improve their social status, as R.C.C. roof houses are considered as a symbol of social status. At the same time those who lived in kutcha and thatched houses are unable to improve their houses. The nature of houses is also depicted in Fig. 6.

Fig. 6: Nature of House

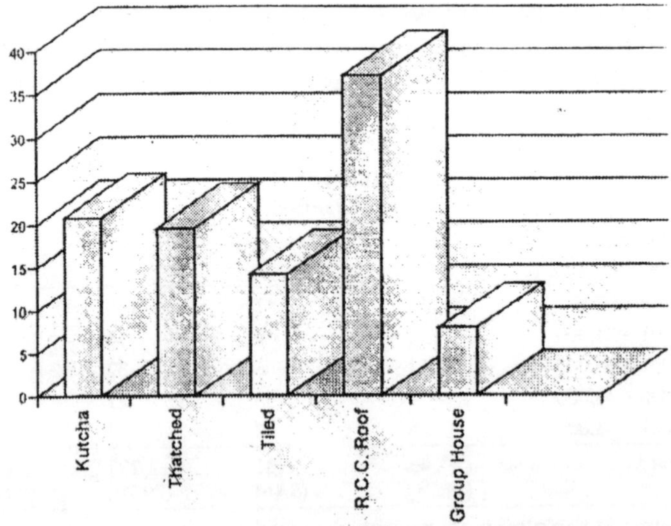

ECONOMIC STATUS

The following aspects are examined for analyzing the economic status of the people of Palamathi hill. They include: the annual income of the households, source of income, ownership of land, sources of irrigation, cropping pattern, value of crops sold, marketing of produce, production of paddy, marketable surplus of paddy, livestock, yield of milk, nature of job, consumption of daily food, expenditure, savings, borrowings and investment.

Assets

Ownership of Land

Land is an important asset for the people in the villages because it is their source of livelihood. The details of ownership of land by the people of Palamathi hill is presented in table 13.

Table 13
Ownership of Land

S. No.	*Income group*	*Land owned (in acres)*						*Total*
		0	*< 1*	*1.1- 2.5*	*2.6 - 3*	*3.1-4*	*> 4*	
1.	Below 12,000	95	71	21	-	2	-	189
2.	12,001 – 24,000	26	25	8	3	2	3	67
3.	24,001 – 36,000	11	26	22	5	5	3	69
4.	36,000 – 48,000	1	13	7	3	2	2	28
5.	48,001 – 64,000	-	3	3	2	1	4	13
	Total	133 (36.33)	138 (37.07)	61 (16.66)	13 (3.60)	12 (3.26)	9 (2.45)	366 (100)

Note: Figures in parenthesis are percentages to the total.

As indicated in the above table, 133 respondents (36.33%) were landless. The remaining 233 respondents (63.66%) owned land. Among the owners of land, the number of respondents decreased with increase in acres of land owned. A little above the landless respondents, 138 respondents (37.07%) owned less than one acre, 61 respondents (16.66%) owned 1.1-2.5acres of land, 13 respondents (3.60%) owned 2.6–3 acres of land while, 12 respondents (3.26%) owned 3.1–4acres of land and only 9 respondents (2.45%) owned >4acres of land. From this it is vivid that there were three categories of farmers viz., landless farmers, marginal farmers and small farmers.

Nature of land Owned

There are three types of land owned by the respondents in Palamathi hill viz., dry, wet and garden lands. The classification of land owned by the respondents is presented in table 14 below.

Table 14
Nature of land owned by the Respondents

S. No.	*Income group*	*Wet*	*Dry*	*Garden*	*Wet & Dry*	*Wet & garden*	*Dry & garden*	*All the three*	*Total*
1.	Below 12,000	14	33	22	4	4	17	3	97
2.	12,001 – 24,000	7	8	15	1	5	5	-	41
3.	24,001 – 36,000	9	8	15	3	6	17	1	59
4.	36,000 – 48,000	2	6	2	3	2	9	2	26
5.	48,001 – 64,000	2	-	3	-	1	4	-	10
	Total	34 (14.59)	55 (23.6)	57 (24.46)	11 (4.72)	18 (7.72)	52 (22.34)	6 (2.57)	233 (100)

Note: Figures in parenthesis are percentages to the total.

As explained in the earlier section of 5.4.1.1, only 233 owned lands. Exclusive wet, dry or garden lands were owned only by 146 respondents, of which 34 (14.59%) had owned wet land, 55 (23.6%) had owned dry land and 57 (24.46%) had owned garden land. The remaining respondents owned one or two combination of these lands. Among them, 11 (4.72%) had owned wet and dry land, 18 (7.42%).

Irrigation

Water is the prime source, which fulfills a number of significant functions. Unlike most natural resources, water does not have a substitute in its main uses. It can be used lavishly or efficiently, but cannot be replaced. Irrigation of water is the most vital and critical input of agricultural production, (Ajit B. Jain, 2002).[2] Irrigation is the artificial application of water to land. Since agriculture is the primary occupation of the inhabitants of Palamathi, it was imperative to analyze the source of irrigation for the crops cultivated. This is depicted in table 20. A large irrigation potential has been created in India, since independence, taking it from 22.6 MHa to over 96.9 MHa. About 40% of the cropped area is irrigated and would further be increased after the projects under construction are completed.[3]

Table 15
Source of Irrigation

S. No.	*Income group*	*Open well*	*Bore well*	*Canal*	*Total*
1.	Below 12,000	53	0	40	93
2.	12,001 – 24,000	17	2	14	33
3.	24,001 – 36,000	41	2	7	50
4.	36,000 – 48,000	20	22	3	45
5.	48,001 – 64,000	8	2	2	12
	Total	139 (59.65)	28 (12.10)	66 (28.32)	233 (100)

Note: Figures in parenthesis are percentages to the total.

Among the various sources of irrigation, open wells were used by 139 farmers, bore wells by 28 farmers and canal by 66 farmers. For the low income group, ie., below Rs. 12,000/- open well and canal are the major sources of irrigation. The bore well were used by higher income groups. Out of the 28 bore wells, 22 belonged to the fourth income group. The remaining 6 bore wells were equally shared by the second, third and fifth income groups.

Livestock

Every farmer in the village possesses livestock in his farm as it supplies milk, manure and employment. Kadirvel (2002), opined that, for small farmers, cattle is perhaps the only tangible asset and mainstay for their socio-economic security.[4]

The value of the livestock ranged between < Rs. 5,000/- to > Rs. 10,000/-, and the livestock was owned only by 195 families. The distribution of livestock based on their value and income of classification of the people is depicted in table 32. The study revealed that 80 families owned livestock that ha value between Rs. 5001/- and Rs. 10,000/-, while 78 families owned livestock that had a value of >Rs. 10,000/-. Only 37 families owned livestock with < Rs. 5,000/-.

Further analysis of the data based on income group indicated that the value of livestock decreased with increase in income level per annum. This may be due to the fact that the poor landless farmers who owned these animals could graze them on open grounds. The people of the lower income group could look after their own animals. It is illustrated in the following table 16.

Table 16
Value of Livestock

S. No.	*Income group*	*Value of Livestock owned (in Rupees)*			*Total*
		< Rs. 5,000	*Rs. 5001 – Rs. 10,000*	*> Rs. 10,000*	
1.	Below 12,000	15	44	33	92
2.	12,001 – 24,000	5	13	14	32
3.	24,001 – 36,000	11	13	18	42
4.	36,000 – 48,000	3	9	7	19
5.	48,001 – 64,000	3	1	6	10
	Total	37	80	78	195 (100)

Note: Figures in parenthesis are percentages to the total.

Vehicles Owned

The inhabitants of Palamathi hills owned a variety of vehicles for personal as well as for the purpose of agricultural production. The types of vehicles ranged from the manual bicycles to the fuel driven types of two wheelers and four wheelers. Agricultural supportive four wheelers included tractors and lorry , while the others were car, moped. Scooter was owned by 6 families while 2 families owned 2 lorries and 2 autos respectively. Tractor and car was owned by one each family. This is illustrated in table 17.

Among the total respondents, 143 (39.97%) had owned vehicles of various types. The bicycles dominated among the vehicles. Of them, 38 belonged to the first group, 20 belonged to the third group and the remaining 10 bicycles are shared by fourth and fifth group respectively.

Table 17
Types of Vehicles owned

S. No.	*Income group*	*Bicycle*	*Scoo-ter*	*Mopeds*	*Auto rickshaw*	*Car*	*Lorry*	*Trac-tor*	*Total*
1.	Below 12,000	38	-	7	1	-	-	-	46
2.	12,001 – 24,000	25	3	11	1	-	-	-	40
3.	24,001 – 36,000	20	1	11	-	-	1	-	33
4.	36,000 – 48,000	4	2	6	-	-	-	-	12
5.	48,001 – 64,000	6	-	3	-	1	1	1	12
	Total	93	6	38	2	1	2	1	143

Source: Primary Data.

There were 44 power driven wheelers, of which 6 were scooters and 38 were mopeds. There were two lorries, two auto's one tractor and one car. The lowest income group had owned 7 mopeds and 1 auto. The scooters are owned by second, third and fourth group. 38 mopeds were shared by all the groups. Two lorries were owned by third and fifth group and one tractor was owned by the fifth group.

Nature of Employment

Out of the sample respondents, 156 (42.62 per cent) were employed as family labour, and they were engaged in their own farms as cultivator, goat rearer etc. 149 respondents (40.71 per cent) were engaged as paid labour. They were working in their land for wages.

Table 18
Nature of Employment

S. No	*Income group*	*Family labour*	*Paid labour*	*Attached labour*	*Family & paid labour*	*Public service*	*Total*
1.	Below 12,000	41	114	7	27	-	189
2.	12,001 – 24,000	34	23	2	7	1	67
3.	24,001 – 36,000	45	12	1	10	1	69
4.	36,000 – 48,000	24	-	-	3	1	28
5.	48,001 – 64,000	12	-	-	-	1	13
	Total	156	149	10	47	4	366

Note: Figures in parenthesis are percentage to total.

10 respondents (2.73 per cent) employed as attached labour on contract. 47 respondents (12.84 per cent) were working as both family and paid labour. The income earned from their own land is insufficient, hence they worked for wages. Only four of the respondents (1.09 per cent) were engaged in public service. The nature of employment reveals that the land owners worked as family labour, whereas, landless labourers were working as paid labour and attached labour. The marginal farmers whose land is less than one acre were doing both family and paid labour.

Cropping Pattern

Area Under Crops

The people in Palamathi are agriculturists. They used the land for cultivation of various crops. The crops grown by the respondents are presented in table 19 below.

Among the various crops, paddy commands the highest area. 49.07 per cent of the area was used for cultivation of paddy. It was followed by Ragi 6.18 per cent area. Among Millets, Cambu and Cholam occupied 13.66 per cent area. The area under pulses accounted for 0.42 per cent. Among Vegetables, Colocassia, Brinjal, Tomato were cultivated predominantly by the respondent farmers. Colocassia accounted for 3.28 per cent of the area, Brinjal accounted for 3.28 per cent of the area, and Tomato accounted for 2.86 per cent of the area. Mango and Banana are the two kinds of fruit trees grown by the respondents. Mango trees accounted for 0.74 per cent of the area and Banana accounted for 6.83 per cent of the area. Spices like Chilli and turmeric accounted for 0.70 per cent and 0.97 per cent respectively of the area. Flower accounted for 0.78 per cent of the area. Among the cash crops, Coconut accounted for 3.26 per cent area, groundnut accounted for 7.91 per cent of the area. Sugarcane was grown in 0.42 per cent of the area.

Thus the farmers in Palamathi hill had given importance to multi crops which were grown both in wet and dry conditions.

Table 19

Cropping Pattern (Total Area of Cultivation of Crops in acres)

S. No.	Income group (Rupees/annum)	Paddy	Millets			Pulses	Vegetables			Fruits		Spices		Flower	Coconut	Ground nut	Sugar cane	Total area (acres)
			Ragi	Cembu	Cholam		Colocasia	Brinjal	Tomato	Mango	Banana	Chili	Turmeric					
1.	Below 12,000	31.1	6.4	9.8	8.15	0.6	-	1.3	2.6	-	3	0.5	-	0.55	-	7.7	-	71.7
2.	12,001 – 24,000	19.45	0.6	1.1	1.1	0.1	0.1	1.2	0.95	-	3.8	0.35	-	0.25	0.5	2.2	1	32.7
3.	24,001 – 36,000	26.25	3.1	2.8	3.65	0.3	1.5	2	1.55	1	5.35	0.8	1.7	0.5	3.70	6.1	-	60.3
4.	36,000 – 48,000	21	3.0	2.75	0.45	-	2	1.75	1.65	0.75	2.5	-	0.6	0.55	-	0.7	-	37.7
5.	48,001 – 64,000	18.2	1.5	2	0.5	-	5	1.5	-	-	1.5	-	-	-	3.5	0.3	-	34
	Total	116	14.6	18.45	13.85	1	8.6	7.75	6.75	1.75	16.15	1.65	2.3	1.85	7.7	17	1	236.7

Source: Primary Data.

Among the various income groups, lowest income group had given highest priority to paddy. Out of the total area of 71.7 acres, paddy was cultivated in 31.1 acres. The third group had cultivated paddy in 26.25 acres as against fourth group which cultivated paddy in 21 acres. It was followed by second group, which cultivated paddy in 19.45 acres and the highest income group had cultivated paddy in 18.2 acres. Thus paddy crop was given primary importance in cultivation by all the income groups in the study area.

Total Value of Produce Sold

The total value of crops cultivated and sold by the inhabitants of Palamathi hills was found to be Rs. 11,22,922.04. The value of individual crops sold is depicted in table 20.

Paddy was found to be the highest yielding crops at the value of Rs. 5,97,215.20, followed by banana yielding a value of Rs. 1,56,905. Coconut and groundnut values were nearly equal giving a sales value of Rs. 57,076/- and Rs. 52,600/- respectively.

Total value of crops sold were further analyzed based on the income group of the inhabitants. The analysis revealed that the highest amount of Rs. 3,12,350.75 was obtained by the people in the income range of Rs. 24,001/- Rs. 36,000/- per annum. This was followed by the people in the lowest income range who obtained a sum of Rs. 2,45,198.25. The 4th and 2nd income range groups received nearly the same amount of Rs. 1,98,312.5 and Rs. 1,94,500.59 respectively. The least was received by the highest income groups. This reveals that the middle income people who invested much in agriculture and depended on agriculture to a great extent received better returns than the others.

Average Value of Crops Sold

The average value of crops was calculated by dividing the total value of each crop by the number of producers of that crop.

As shown in the above table, the average value of crops sold by respondents had increased with the size of groups. In the case of paddy, the average value obtained by the first group

Table 20
Total Value of Crops Sold (In Rupees)

S. No	Income group (Rupees/ annum)	Sale of crops (Rupees) Paddy	Ragi	Cambu	Cholam	Pulses	Colo-casia	Brinjal	Tomato	Mango	Banana	Chili	Tur-meric	Flower	Coconut	Ground nut	Sugar cane	Total
1.	Below 12,000	1,49,626.25	9,225	11,070	1,400	4,080	-	8,460	6,342	-	20,125	2,300	-	11,220	-	21,350	-	2,45,198.25
2.	12,001–24,000	1,07,725.75	2,925	2,160	2,200	-	600	4,675	2,340	7,200	31,465	1,200	-	6,300	7,800	7,500	1,0,409.84	1,94,500.59
3.	24,001–36,000	12,705.75	9,450	3,000	5,200	1,284	12,000	5,600	3,255	-	66,290	3,340	12,500	18,000	22,276	22,250	-	3,12,350.75
4.	36,000–48,000	1,17,081.50	6,300	3,270	1,200	-	15,000	7,550	3,480	7,440	17,500	-	6,500	12,000	-	1,000	-	1,98,321.5
5.	48,001–64,000	94,875.95	4,950	-	2,400	-	16,800	4,500	-	-	21,525	-	-	-	27,000	500	-	1,72,550.95
	Total	5,97,215.20	32,850	19,500	12,400	5,364	44,400	30,785	15,417	14,640	156,905	6,840	19,000	47,520	57,076	52,600	1,0,409.84	11,22,922.04

Source: Primary Data.

Table 21
Average Value of Crops Sold (In Rupees)

S. No	Income group (Rupees/ annum)	Sale of crops (Rupees) Paddy	Ragi	Cambu	Cholam	Pulses	Colo-casia	Brinjal	Tomato	Mango	Banana	Chili	Tur-meric	Flower	Coconut	Ground nut	Sugar cane	Total area (acres)
1.	Below 12,000	2,823.14	576.56	503.18	466.66	2040	-	650	906	-	5,031.25	2300	-	5610	-	1,067.50	-	21,974.29
2.	12,001–24,000	3,264.41	975	540	733.33	-	300	667.85	780	7,200	5244.16	1200	-	6,300	7,800	1,875	10,409.84	47,289.59
3.	24,001–36,000	3,761.93	1,050	428.57	520	1284	6000	800	813.75	-	6,629	1670	2,500	18,000	7,425.33	1589.28	-	52,471.86
4.	36,000–48,000	5,575.30	1,260	8,175	600	-	7500	7258.33	870	3,720	8750	-	3,250	6,000	-	1000	-	47,958.63
5.	48,001–64,000	10,541.77	1,650	-	2,400	-	5600	4500	-	-	10,762.5	-	-	-	6,750	500	-	42,704.27
	Total	25,966.55	5,511.56	9,646.75	4,719	3324	19,400	7,876.18	3369.75	10,920	36,416.91	5170	5,750	35,910	2,197.33	6,031.78	10,409.84	2,12,398.64

Source: Primary Data.

of farmers was only Rs. 2,823.14. The average value increases with the size of farms from second group to fifth group. This is due to distress sale of crop by the small producers of paddy. The same trend can be noticed in the case of ragi also.

In the case of Cambu and Cholam the third group and second group respectively had received lower average value compared to the other groups. Pulse was grown by only one group. In the case of Colocassia , fifth group had secured lower average value compared to the fourth group. Similar trend can be noticed in the case of vegetables like Brinjal. In the case of Tomato, the first group has secured higher average price compared to the other three group.

Among the fruits, second group has secured higher price compared to the fourth group. In the case of banana, the average value has increased with size of farms. In the case of spices, first group has secured higher price than the second and third group. The average value for turmeric has increased with size of farms. In the case of flowers, third and fourth groups secured higher average value than the first and fourth group. Second group has secured higher average price for coconut compared to third and fifth groups. In the case of groundnut second group has secured higher price compared to other groups. There is only one producer of sugarcane.

Production of Paddy

Total and Average Production of Paddy

Paddy being a staple food crop, it is grown by many farmers. The inhabitants of the Palamathi hills, irrespective of income group, had cultivated paddy. As shown in table 22, the smallest farms have produced largest quantity of 364.79 quintals of paddy.

It was followed by the third income group that produced 302.84 quintals. The second, fourth and fifth income groups had recorded a production of 270.6 quintals, 260.13 quintals and 168.9 quintals respectively.

Though the small farms could produce highest total quantity of paddy, they are the least in average production.

The total quantity of paddy, they are the least in average production. The total production is high in the group because of large number of farms.

Table 22
Total Production and Average Production of Paddy

S. No.	*Income group*	*Production of Paddy (Qtly)*		
		Number of producers	*Total production*	*Average production*
1.	Below 12,000	53	364.79	6.88
2.	12,001 – 24,000	33	270.60	8.20
3.	24,001 – 36,000	34	302.84	8.90
4.	36,000 – 48,000	21	260.23	12.39
5.	48,001 – 64,000	9	168.90	18.76
	Total	150	1,367.36	55.13

Source: Primary Data.

But average production has increased with the increase in the size of farms. The average production of paddy in second group was 8.20 quintals, third group 8.90 quintals, fourth group 12.39 quintals and the fifth group could produce 18.76 quintals. Since the average production of paddy is large in big farms, the large farms can be considered as efficient in production as recorded by the 5th income group

Marketed Surplus of Paddy

Marketed surplus is the actual quantity sold in the market by the farmers. The marketed surplus is calculated by subtracting the quantity consumed and the quantity retained for seed purposes by the farmers from the total production. Table 23 provides the marketed surplus of paddy or the quantity sold by the respondent farmers.

The first group had marketed 182.10 quintals (49.92 per cent) of the total production. The second group could market 59.70 quintals (16.31 per cent). The third group had marketed 193.55 quintals which formed 63.91 per cent of the total production. The fourth group marketed 172.48 quintals (66.28 per cent) of the total production. The last group had marketed 116.50 quintals (68.98 per cent)of the total production. The quantity sold by all the farms is calculated as 724.33, which formed 52.97 per cent of the total production.

Table 23
Marketed Surplus of Paddy

S. No.	*Income group*	*Number of producers*	*Total production*	*Quantity consumed (quintals)*	*Quantity sold (marketed surplus in quintals)*	*Per cent (%)*
1.	Below 12,000	53	364.79	182.69	182.10	49.92
2.	12,001 – 24,000	33	270.60	210.90	59.70	16.31
3.	24,001 – 36,000	34	302.84	109.29	193.55	63.91
4.	36,000 – 48,000	21	260.23	87.75	172.48	66.28
5.	48,001 – 64,000	9	168.90	52.41	116.50	68.98
	Total	150	1,367.36	643.04	724.33	52.97

Source: Primary Data.

Though the total production is large in small farms, they consumed more. Therefore, they could sell only 50 per cent of their production. The smallest quantity is marketed by the second group, which is accounted for 59.70 quintals (16.31 per cent). The remaining groups had contributed higher percentage of their produce. Therefore, it can be concluded that large farms could generate more marketed surplus than the small farms.

Correlation Matrix of Variables

A correlation matrix was done to describe the relationship among the variables, marketed surplus, net area, output, family size, consumption and expenditure. The result of the matrix is provided below. It is illustrated in table 24.

As displayed in the above table, marketed surplus is positively correlated with net area and it is highly significant. The net area is positively correlated with output, consumption and expenditure. As net area increases, the output, consumption and expenditure also increase. Or as net area decreases, the output, consumption and expenditure also decrease.

The variable output is positively correlated with family size, consumption and expenditure. As family size increases, output also increases, and as output increases or decreases, the consumption and expenditure also increases or decreases.

Table 24
Correlation Matrix of Variables

S. No.	*Variables*	*Market-able*	*Net area*	*Output*	*Family size*	*Consum-ption*	*Expen-diture*
1.	Marketable	1.000	.266**				
2.	Net area		1.000	.338**		.163**	.308*
3.	Output			1.000	.289*	.566**	.595**
4.	Family size				1.000	.164*	.213**
5.	Consumption					1.000	.172*
6.	Expenditure						1.000

* Correlation is significant at 0.05 level; **correlation is significant at 0.01 level.

The variable family size, is positively correlated with consumption. As family size increases, the consumption also increases. Or as family size decreases, the consumption also decreases.

Finally, the variable, consumption is positively correlated with expenditure. As consumption increases or decreases, the expenditure also increases or decreases.

Regression Analysis on Marketable Surplus

Regression analysis has been done to predict the marketable surplus from its related variables. The stepwise procedure is used in the analysis to arrive at the regression equation. The following table 25 gives the details of the analysis.

Table 25
Regression Analysis for Dependent Variable, Marketed Surplus

Variables	β	*'t' value*	*Sig*
Net area	.260	3.242	.001
Output	-.050	-.623	.534
Family size	-.029	-.358	.721
Price of paddy	.125	1.507	.134

Constant = 352.855 t = 20.918 P.01.
F =10.509, DF = 1,P.01, R Square = .068

The following variables are introduced in the regression model: net area, output, family size, and price of paddy. The initial screening procedure under stepwise regression method has eliminated output, family size and price of paddy from the regression model since their 't' values were not significant. The remaining variables are fitted into regression model.

Marketed surplus is considered as dependent variable. The independent variable, net area, has been used in the model to predict the dependent variable.

Net area plays a predominant role in predicting the marketed surplus. The 't' value is 3.242 and Beta value is 260. Both the values are higher. So the net area is the strongest predictor of the four variables introduced.

The 'F' value is significant (F = 10.509, ef = 1, P 0.01) and this indicates that the regression equation predicts the dependent variable at greater level. The constant value 352.855 is statistically significant (t =20,918 P0.01).

Marketing of Produce

Market plays an important role in the development of agriculture by securing fair return to the farmer for his produce, making available to him all the required inputs, and by providing him the required information. The market creates space, form and time utility to the produce. The value of a commodity depends on where the produce is sold. How the respondents of Palamathi hills dispose of their farm produce and their response are recorded and presented in Table 26 below.

Table 26
Marketing of Produce

S. No.	*Income group*	*Local*	*Vellore*	*Salem*	*Total*
1.	Below 12,000	2	92	1	95
2.	12,001 – 24,000	1	40	-	41
3.	24,001 – 36,000	1	48	5	54
4.	36,000 – 48,000	3	23	2	28
5.	48,001 – 64,000	-	12	1	13
	Total	7 (3.03)	215 (93.07)	9 (3.9)	231 (100)

Note: Figures in parenthesis are percentage to total.

The farm produces were sold by the respondents at Palamathi itself or Vellore market or at Salem. Only 7 respondents (3.03 per cent) had chosen to sell their produce at Palamathi hills. The itinerant merchants visit the villages and make purchases after paying very low price.

On the other hand, 215 (93.07 per cent) respondents had sold their produce at Vellore market, which is 8 kilometers away from the Palamathi hills. Vellore has a well established market, managed by private as well as regulated market. The respondents sold all their products at the Vellore market in spite of transport problems and other malpractices in the market.

Few respondents 9 (3.9 per cent) had taken their produce to Salem for sale. There are some special markets for sale of turmeric and other spices at Salem. Though few in number, the farmers at Palamathi were aware of the advantage of selling their produce at Salem.

Income

Source of Income

The disaggregation of annual income is presented in Table 27 below.

Of the total income of 62,32,094.30, 41,63,513.90 (66.80 per cent) was received from wages. It was followed by Rs. 10,35,616.10 received from the sale of crops. Sale of milk, which accounted for Rs. 4,32,134.39 (6.93 per cent) formed third position. Other sources which accounted for Rs. 3,51,512.23 (5.65 per cent) ranked fourth in its contribution towards the annual income. Sale of animals which contributed Rs. 2,49,316.81 (4.0 per cent) towards gross income is in the last place.

Income from Wages

Income from wages formed an important component of gross income of the respondents in Palamathi hills during the year of survey. The first group had contributed Rs.17,22,572.90 as wages, which formed nearly 41.73 per cent to the total wages. This is due to the fact that majority of the wage earners (78

Table 27
Disaggregation of Annual Income

S. No.	Income group	Sources of income: Sale of crops	Sale of animals	Sale of milk	Wages received	Other sources	Total
1.	Below 12,000	2,75,284.30	56,910.00	44,770	17,22,572.90	22,000	2,121,537.20
2.	12,001 – 24,000	2,10,052.01	49,474.85	60,124.89	6,98,585.56	45,474.89	1,063,712.10
3.	24,001 – 36,000	1,90,607.15	99,132	1,92,532.04	9,99,137.90	71,467.12	1,551,926.10
4.	36,000 – 48,000	1.82,338.74	25,799.96	81,194.96	6,01,464.16	89,078.32	979,876.14
5.	48,001 – 64,000	1,77,333.99	18,000	53,512.50	1,41,704.50	1,23,491.90	514,042.89
	Total	10,35,616.10 (16.62)	2,49,316.81 (4.00)	4,32,134.39 (6.93)	41,63.513.90 (66.80)	3,51,512.23 (5.65)	62,32,094.30 (100)

Source: Estimated from the primary data collected from the households.
Note: Figures in parenthesis are percentage to total.

coolies) belonged to the first group. It was followed by third group, who contributed Rs. 99,99,187.90 towards wage. The second group had contributed Rs. 6,98,585.56, fourth group had contributed Rs. 6,01,464.16 and the fifth group had contributed Rs.1,41,704.50 towards wage.

Income from Sale of Crops

Income from sale of crops is the second major components of gross income. The distribution of income from sale of crops to various income groups shows that the first group accounted for 26.61 per cent, followed by second group, which accounted for 20.28 per cent, followed by the third, fourth and fifth groups in the ratio of 18.41 per cent, 17.61 per cent and 17.12 per cent respectively.

Income from the Sale of Milk

The income from the sale of milk forms the third important component of the gross income. The third important component of the gross income. The third group accounted for the major contribution. It contributed Rs. 1,92,532.04, which formed 3.09 per cent. It was followed by the fourth group, which accounted for Rs. 81,194.96 (1.30 per cent), second group had contributed Rs. 60.124.89 (0.96 per cent), fifth group's contribution was to Rs. 53,512.50 (0.86 per cent) and the first group contribution was Rs. 44,770.00 (0.72 per cent).

Income from the Sale of Animals

Invariably, almost all the respondents keep goats for rearing. When the goats are sold, it forms the income of the family. Third group accounted for the major contribution. It contributed Rs. 1,92,532.04, which formed 3.09 per cent. It was followed by the fourth group, which accounted for Rs. 81,194.96 (1.30 per cent)second group had contributed Rs. 60.124.89 (0.96 per cent), fifth group's contribution was toRs. 53,512.50 (0.86 per cent) and the first group contribution was Rs. 53,512.50 (0.86 per cent) and the first group contribution was Rs. 44,770.00 (0.72 per cent).

Income from the Sale of Animals

Invariably, almost all the respondents keep goats for rearing. When the goats are sold, it forms the income of the family. Third group has contributed largest amount Rs. 99,132.00 (1.59 per cent) towards total income. It was followed by first group, second group, fourth group and fifth group.

Income Earned from other Sources

In this item, fifth group stands first with Rs. 1,23,491.90 as against fourth group with its contribution of Rs. 89,078.32, third group's contribution of Rs. 71,467.12, second group contribution of Rs. 45,474.89 and first group contribution of Rs. 22,000.00 respectively.

Annual Expenditure

Item-wise Annual Expenditure

Total Expenditure

The total annual expenditure and the item-wise annual expenditure done by the respondents are presented in Table 28.

The total expenditure incurred by all the groups has been estimated as Rs. 54,62,100.83. The distribution of total expenditure among various groups shows that the first group has incurred the highest expenditure of Rs. 16,81849.678 (30.81per cent), followed by third group Rs. 14,61,593.63 (26.75 per cent), second group Rs. 10,77,850.20 (19.73 per cent), fourth group Rs. 6,93.350.68 (12.69per cent), and the last group Rs. 5,47,456.65 (10.02 per cent)

Expenditure on Food

Among the various items of expenditure, expenditure on food stands first with Rs. 35,70,139.01 (65.36 per cent) The pattern of expenditure reveals that the first group had spent largest amount than other groups. It was followed by third group, second group, fourth group and fifth group. As it is generally noticed, the lower income group spends major share of their income on food compared to higher income groups.

Table 28
Item wise Annual Expenditure (in Rupees)

S. No.	Income group (Rupees/annum)	Annual expenditure								Total
		Food	Beverage	Entertainment	Medicine	Electricity	Transport	Festival	Clothing	
1.	Below 12,000	12,81,750.00	I,29,477.78	52,269.18	29,427.73	39,283.73	33,605.20	28,856.40	87,179.65	16,81,849.67
2.	12,001 – 24,000	6,13,980.63	1,01,125.74	65,521.43	56,804.58	51,189.45	52,814.85	56,436.85	79,976.67	10,77,850.20
3.	24,001 – 36,000	10,09,585.90	1,07,725.00	66,803.51	58,904.58	5,821.00	61,900.12	62,934.85	87,918.4	14,61,593
4.	36,000 – 48,000	4,10,540.19	74,520.38	23,380.39	27,955.19	32,654.33	22,640.19	40,771.81	60,888.20	6,93,350.68
5.	48,001 – 64,000	2,54,282.29	64,051.00	75,166.00	39,720.85	12,184.51	24,156.00	32,500.00	45,396.00	5,47,456.65
	Total	35,70,139.01 (65.36)	4,76,899.9 (8.73)	2,83,140.506 (5.18)	2,12,812.93 (3.89)	1,41,133.0.15 (2.58)	1,95,116.36 (3.57)	2,21,499.91 (4.05)	3,61,359.19 (6.61)	54,62,100.20 (100.00)

Source: Primary data.
Note: Figures in parenthesis are percentage to total.

Expenditure on Beverages

Expenditure on beverages formed 8.73 per cent of the total expenditure. Highest expenditure in beverages was made by the first group, followed by third group, second, fourth and fifth groups respectively.

Expenditure on Entertainment

Expenditure on entertainment formed 5.18 per cent. Among the groups had spent highest amount on entertainment compared to other groups.

Expenditure on Medicine

Expenditure on medicine accounted for 3.89 per cent of the total expenditure. Highest amount of expenditure on medicine was made by the third group, followed by second group, fifth group, first and fourth group respectively.

Expenditure on Cloths

Expenditure on cloths formed the third largest items of expenditure with 6.61 per cent of the total expenditure. Group wise highest expenditure on festival was made by the third and second group followed by the first, fourth and fifth groups.

Expenditure on Festivals

The fourth major item of expenditure is on festivals which formed 4.05 per cent of the total expenditure. The highest expenditure on festival was made by third and second group followed by the fourth, fifth and first groups.

Expenditure on Transport

Since the hill people have to travel frequently to town or Vellore. They have to spend sizeable amount on travel to Vellore. They have to spend sizeable amount on travel, which formed 4.05 per cent of the total expenditure. The highest expenditure on travel was made by the third group followed by the second, first, fifth and fourth group respectively.

Expenditure on Electricity

Last item of expenditure incurred by the respondents was on electricity which formed 2.58 per cent of the total expenditure. Highest amount of expenditure on electricity was made by the second group, followed by first , fourth, fifth and third group respectively.

Expenditure on Electricity

Last item of expenditure incurred by the respondents was on electricity which formed 2.58 per cent of the total expenditure. Highest amount of expenditure on electricity was made by the second group, followed by first, fourth, fifth and third group respectively.

Hamlet wise Classification of Annual Expenditure

Hamlet wise classification of annual expenditure shows that Changanatham hamlet had spent highest amount of 19,84,500.00 (36.33 per cent) because of highest number of respondents in this hamlet (see Table 29). It was followed by Palamathi (23.18 per cent), Setari (16.94 per cent), Arasankulam (15.33 per cent) and Krishnapuram (8.22per cent) respectively.

Comparison of Annual Income and Expenditure

The comparison of total annual income and expenditure shows surplus of income over expenditure in all the groups, But the surplus varies from group to group. The surplus of income over expenditure in the first group was calculated as Rs. 1,37,037.10 (6.45 per cent). In the second group , the surplus income was Rs. 2,25,971.20 (21.24 per cent), in the third group, the surplus income was Rs. 2,86,776.10 (18.46 per cent), the fourth group had recorded a surplus of Rs. 54,425.94 (5.55 per cent) and the surplus in fifth group was Rs. 7,69993.10 (12.35 per cent). The highest net income over expenditure was generated by the second group followed by third group. The richest groups have generated smaller net income.

The group wise annual income and expenditure is presented in table 30.

Table 29
Hamlet Wise Classification of Annual Expenditure

S. No.	Names of Hamlets	Income Group					Total
		Below 12,000	12,001 –24,000	24,001–36,000	36,000 – 48,000	48,001 – 64,000	
1.	Chenganatham (134)	793800.00	299321.00	476125.00	239879.00	175375.00	19,84,500.00
2.	Palamathi (112)	434550.00	218130.00	278120.00	182120.00	153230.00	12,66,150.00
3.	Setari (73)	346919.40	185170.72	200080.00	108190.04	85090.04	9,25,450.20
4.	Arasankulam (22)	-	282108.54	386268.21	85061.644	84061.614	8,37,500.00
5.	Krishnapuram (25)	106580.00	93120.02	121000.00	78100.00	49700.00	4,48,500.02
	Total (366)	1681849.40 (30.79)	1077850.20 (19.73)	1461593.40 (26.75)	693350.68 (12.71)	547456.65 (10.02)	54,62,100.20 (100.00)

Note: Figures in parenthesis are percentage to total.

Table 30
Comparison of Annual Income and Expenditure

S. No.	Income group	Annual Income (Rs.)	Annual Expenditure (Rs.)	Difference (Rs)
1.	Below 12,000	21,21537.10	19,84,500.00	+1,37,037.10
2.	12,001 – 24,000	10634711.20	8,37,500.00	+2,25,971.20
3.	24,001 – 36,000	1552926.10	12,66,150.00	+2,86,776.10
4.	36,000 – 48,000	979876.14	9,25,450.20	+54,425.94
5.	48,001 – 64,000	514042.89	4,48,500.00	+65,542.88
	Total	6232093.30	5462100.20	+79,993.10

Correlation Method for Finding the Relationship between Income and Expenditure

For finding the relationship between income and expenditure of the inhabitants of Palamathi Hills, Correlation Method is used.

$$r = \frac{\Sigma xy}{\sqrt{\Sigma x^2 \times \Sigma y^2}}$$

Where,

r = correlation

Σxy= sum of xy value

Σx^2 = sum of x^2 value

Σy^2 = sum of y^2 value

X	X-X x	X^2	Y	Y-5 Y	Y^2	XY
21.21	8.76	76.73	19.84	8.92	79.56	78.13
10.63	-1.82	3.31	8.37	-2.55	6.50	4.64
15.52	3.07	9.42	12.66	1.74	3.02	5.34
9.79	-2.66	7.07	9.25	- 1.67	2.78	4.44
5.14	-7.31	53.43	4.48	- 6.44	41.47	47.07
$\Sigma x = 62.29$	$\Sigma x = 0.04$	Σx^2 149.96	54.6	0	133.3	139.62

$$r = \frac{\Sigma xy}{\sqrt{\Sigma x^2 \times \Sigma y^2}}$$

$$r = \frac{139.62}{\sqrt{149.96 \times 133.3}}$$

$$r = \frac{139.62}{\sqrt{19989.6}}$$

$$r = \frac{139.62}{\sqrt{141.38}}$$

$$r = 0.98$$

Result

Very high degree of positive correlation between the income and expenditure of the respondents in Palamathi hills is found.

Savings

Saving is the difference between income and expenditure. Those who saved are moving towards prosperity. Only 26 respondents (7.10 per cent) could save. The distribution of those who saved among various groups shows that there are 14 respondents belonging to third group, three each belonged to the remaining group. It is therefore, necessary to find out, "how much they saved" and "where they had saved".

Quantum of Saving

The quantum of saving given in table 31 shows that there are three respondents who saved less than Rs. 500, six respondents saved between Rs. 5,001 to 15,000, five respondents saved between Rs. 35,000 to 45,000, three respondents saved between Rs. 45,001 to 55,000 and one respondent saved between Rs. 55,001 to 65,000.

Sources of Saving

"Where saved?" is as much important as " how much is saved?" A majority of 13 of the respondents (50 per cent) had saved with banks, which is an encouraging trend in the rural area particularly in Palamathi hills. Only one respondent had deposited with cooperative society. It shows that the co-operatives are not popular in the study area.

Table 31
Quantum of Savings

S. No.	Income group	Below 5000	5,001 to 15,00	15,001 to 25,000	25,001 to 35,000	35,001 to 45,000	45,001 to 55,000	65,000 to 75,000	Total
1.	Below 12,000	-	2	-	1	-	-	-	3
2.	12,001 – 24,000	1	1	1	-	-	-	-	3
3.	24,001 – 36,000	2	1	2	4	3	2	-	14
4.	36,000 – 48,000	-	1	1	-	1	-	-	3
5.	48,001 – 64,000	-	1	-	-	-	1	1	3
	Total	3	6	4	5	4	3	1	26
		11.53	1.64	1.97	1.81	1.09	11.053	3.80	100.00

Note: Figures in parenthesis are percentage to total.

Seven of the respondents had saved with private financers and relatives dominate in the mobilization of savings of the people of Palamathi hills.

Borrowing

Rural indebtness has taken deep roots in the country and hence constitutes a serious economic, social and political problems for the Indian economy. The mounting burden of rural debt has crippled the rural economy. The magnitude of rural indebtness is increasing year after year due to poor capacity of the rural people to pay off their old debts which may be attributed to a host of forces such as low production, high interest rates etc.[5]

Quantum of Borrowing

Debt was not an exception for the people of Palamathi. They too had debts from below Rs. 5,000/-to above Rs. 25,000/-. There were a total of 187 households that had debts. The study revealed that 33/16 per cent had a debt of Rs. 5,001-Rs. 10,000 while 26.74 per cent had a debt below Rs. 5,000, However, 17.65 per cent had a debt in the range of Rs. 5,001 to Rs. 10,000/- and recorded to be the highest. The next highest of 13.37 per cent was found below Rs. 5,000/-. It is worth mentioning that both these highest percentages were among the lowest income group.

Further analysis of the table in terms of the income group revealed that 47.59 per cent had debts in the first income group. With increase in income, the number of borrowers decreased. There were also no borrowers in the 4th and 5th income group between the debt range of Rs. 10,001 to Rs. 25,000/- The details are furnished in table 32.

Table 32
Quantum of Borrowing

S. No.	*Income group*	*Below 5000*	*5001– 10,000*	*10,001– 15,000*	*15,001– 20,000*	*20,001– 25,000*	*>25,000*	*Total*
1.	Below 12,000	25	29	6	10	4	15	89
2.	12,001 – 24,000	8	16	2	4	1	7	38
3.	24,001 – 36,000	7	8	7	3	2	5	32
4.	36,000 – 48,000	9	6	1	1	-	3	20
5.	48,001 – 64,000	1	3	-	-	1	3	8
	Total	50 (26.74)	62 (33.16)	16 (8.56)	18 (9.63)	8 (4.28)	33 (17.65)	187 (100.00)

Note: Figures in parenthesis are percentage to total.

Sources of Borrowing

Out of the 187 borrowers, 83 of them (44.35 per cent) had borrowed from money lenders (table 33). Relatives accounted for 23.52 per cent of the borrowing. It was followed by banks, which accounted for 12.23 per cent. The respondents had borrowed from more than one source.

Two respondents had borrowed from traders and cooperatives. Another two respondents had borrowed from cooperatives and moneylenders. Four respondents had borrowed from banks and relatives. Three respondents had borrowed from cooperatives and relatives. Two each of the respondents had borrowed from money lenders and relatives, and banks and cooperatives and one respondent had borrowed both from institutional and non-institutional sources. Non-institutional sources dominate over the institutions. It is necessary to strengthen the institutional advances to the people of Palamathi hills.

Table 33
Sources of Borrowings

S. No.	Income group	Banks	Coopera-tives	Traders	Money lender	Rela-tives	Traders & coope-ratives	Coope-ratives & money lenders	Banks & rela-tives	Coope-rative & Rela-tives	Money lenders & Relatives	Traders & Rela-tives	Banks & Cooper-atives	Total
1.	Below 12,000	13	10	1	39	20	-	1	-	1	2	-	2	89
2.	12,001 – 24,000	4	1	2	17	12	-	-	2	-	-	-	-	38
3.	24,001 – 36,000	5	4	1	12	8	-	-	-	1	-	1	-	32
4.	36,000 – 48,000	1	2	1	11	3	-	1	1	1	-	-	-	20
5.	48,001 – 64,000	-	-	-	4	1	1	-	1	1	-	-	-	8
Total		23 (12.29)	17 (9.17)	5 (2.67)	83 (44..38)	44 (23.52)	1 (0..53)	2 (1.06)	4 (2.13)	3 (1.60)	2 (1.06)	1 (0.53)	2 (1.06)	187 (100)

Note: Figures in parenthesis are percentage to total.

Purpose of Borrowing

The purpose of borrowing varies with respondents. The borrowers were classified according to the purpose of borrowing and presented in table 34.

Table 34
Purpose of Borrowing

S. No	*Purpose of Borrowing*	*No of respondents*
1.	Family expenditure	19
2.	Buying cow	17
3.	House construction	50
4.	Marriage	24
5.	Agriculture	25
6.	Digging Well	13
7.	Ear piercing	1
8.	Buying land	5
9.	House construction and Marriage	5
10.	Buying TV	1
11.	House maintenance	2
12.	Buying auto	2
13.	Buying cow and house repairing	3
14.	Electricity construction	1
15.	Buying goat	7
16.	Medical expenses	7
17.	Business needs	1
18.	Digging of well	2
19.	Digging well for agriculture	1
20.	Buying cow and goat	2
21.	House construction and digging of well	1
	Total	187

Source: Primary Data.

The purpose of borrowing are divided into borrowing for productive purposes and borrowing for unproductive purposes. Out of the 87 borrowers, 45 of them (24.06 per cent) had borrowed for unproductive purposes like consumption, marriage, ear boring and for the purchase of television. The remaining borrowers had borrowed for productive purposes like, buying cows, house construction, agriculture, digging well, buying land, house repair, electricity connection, buying goat, meeting medical expense, business, deepening well etc.

Those who borrowed for unproductive purposes should be discouraged so that their repaying capacity could be strengthened.

Investment

Economic analysis of any group is not complete without the study of investment. 50 respondents among 366 could make investments. 28 per cent of the investors belonged to third group. 10 each investors (20 per cent) belonged to first group, second group and fifth group. Six investors (12 per cent) which belonged to fourth group had made investment, and it is depicted in table 35.

Table 35
Investment

S. No.	*Income group*	*< 25,000*	*25,001-50,000*	*50,001-1,00,000*	*1,00,001-2,00,000*	*Total*
1.	Below 12,000	9	1	-	-	10
2.	12,001 – 24,000	1	8	1	-	10
3.	24,001 – 36,000	2	7	1	4	14
4.	36,000 – 48,000	-	2	4	-	6
5.	48,001 – 64,000	-	9	1	-	10
	Total	12 (24.00)	27 (54.00)	7 (14.00)	4 (8.00)	50 (100.00)

Note: Figures in parenthesis are per centage to total.

Regarding the quantum of investment among the investors, 12 respondents (24 per cent) had invested below Rs. 25,000, 27 respondents (54 per cent) had invested 25,001 to 50,000, seven respondents (14 per cent) had invested between Rs. 50,001 to 1,00,000 and four respondents had invested more than one lakh rupees. Since the number of investors are very small, it is necessary to encourage the respondents to invest by giving them adequate incentives.

POVERTY IN PALAMATHI

It is one of the objectives of the present study to analyze poverty prevailing among the people in Palamathi. Poverty is analyzed in terms of annual income , households included in Below the Poverty List (BPL) and child labour.

Poverty of Income

The households were classified according to annual income. There are 189 respondents in the first group whose annual income was below Rs .12,000. Therefore, all the households with an annual income of less than Rs.12,000, have been taken as households living below the poverty list as indicated in table 1.

Poverty of Assets

Majority of the respondents , who are from the first group, were landless labourers. They were coolies, undertaking paid jobs. Except wages, they had no other sources of income.

Scheduled Caste and Other Weaker Section

Out of the 189 respondents, 17 respondents belonged to scheduled caste and 140 respondents belonged to weaker section (see table 36). Scheduled Caste respondents did not own land or any other assets. Similarly, the weaker section do not have adequate assets or income for their existence.

Table 36
Scheduled Caste and other Weaker Section

S. No.	*Hamlet*	*Scheduled caste*	*Other caste*	*Total*
1.	Chenganatham	18	53	71
2.	Krishnapuram	-	3	3
3.	Arasankulam	-	17	17
4.	Palamathi	-	88	88
5.	Chettari	9	1	10
	Total	27	162	189

Child Labourers

The problem of child labour is predominant in some parts of Vellore District and Palamathi is no exception to it. The district has many industries. Child labourers were found in 43 families and comprise both sexes in the age ranging between 5-14 years. The number of child labourers decreased from 28 in the income range of <12,000 rupees per year to 11 in the income range of 12,001-24,000 rupees per year to 4 in the income range of 24,001-

36,000 rupees per year. Child labourers were nil in the next two higher income range groups. Male child labourers were more than female child labourers. The highest child labourers were males in the range of 11-14 years, in the first income group recording 12 children. The next highest child labourers (8) were also males in the age range of 6-10 years. There were no female child labourers in the age range of <5years in any income group, except for 1 male child labourer in each of the income group of <12,000 and 12,001-24,000 rupees per year. This is depicted in the following table 37.

Table 37
Child Labourers in the House Holds

S. No.	Income group	Below 5 yrs		6 - 10 yrs		11 - 14 yrs		Total
		Male	Female	Male	Female	Male	Female	
1.	Below 12,000	1	-	8	5	12	2	28
2.	12,001 – 24,000	1	-	4	-	6	-	11
3.	24,001 – 36,000	-	-	1	-	3	-	4
4.	36,000 – 48,000	-	-	-	-	-	-	-
5.	48,001 – 64,000	-	-	-	-	-	-	-
	Total	2	-	13	5	21	2	43

Source: Primary data.

Basic Amenities

Basic amenities available to the respondents would determine the level of living. Out of the 366 respondents, 223 respondents (60.90 per cent) had tap water. Bore water was used by 89 respondents (23.50). 54 respondents (14.80 per cent) had utilized well water, 220 respondents (60.10 per cent) had electricity connections, 40 per cent of the respondents could not avail electricity connections. But nineteen households were yet to receive electric connection. Palamathi is an eye opener to this fact that households remain unconnected with electricity.

Sanitation is another area, which the respondents of Palamathi hills were lacking. 359 respondents (98.08 per cent) were accessible to dry latrines. On the other hand, 7 respondents (1.92 per cent) only had accessibility to wet latrines.

Table 38
Basic Amenities

S. No	*Income group*	*Tap water*	*Bore water*	*Well water*	*Electricity Connection*	*Sanitation Dry*	*Sanitation Wet*	*Waste Disposal Pit*	*Waste Disposal Open*
1.	Below 12,000	125	48	21	108	188	1	-	189
2.	12,001 – 24,000	39	14	8	41	66	1	-	67
3.	24,001 – 36,000	38	18	13	42	66	3	-	69
4.	36,000 – 48,000	16	5	6	18	27	1	-	28
5.	48,001 – 64,000	5	4	6	11	12	1	-	13
	Total	223	89	54	220	359	7		
		(60.90)	(23.50)	(14.80)	(60.10)	(98.10)	(1. 90)	-	366

Source: Primary Data.
Note: Figures in Parenthesis are percentage to total.

DEVELOPMENT PROGRAMS UNDERTAKEN IN PALAMATHI HILL

In pursuance of the policy of development of hill regions, the Government has launched various program to develop Palamathi hill. These programs can be classified as general programs and specific programs.

General Programs

State Financial Commission, subsidy for works, employment guarantee scheme, constituency development and through M.P., and constituency development fund through M.L.A., underdeveloped Panchayat scheme, Equalization and Motivation subsidy finance and establishment of Tourism Development Centre, Parliamentary Constituency Development Fund, and Namaku Namay Thitam, are the general programs.

Specific Programs

Jawahar Rozgar Yojana, Indira Memorial Housing Scheme, Highway Maintenance and renovation, Drought Prone Area program, Tamilnadu Forest Development Scheme, are the specific programs.

The aim of these programs is to ameliorate the living condition of the hill people, create basic facilities, strengthen the productive capacity, promote institutions and protect the environment.

How far did these programs change the life of the people in Palamathi hill? This question is analyzed by throwing light on the benefits received, both direct and indirect, by the inhabitants of Palamathi hills.

Direct Benefit

Various assistance received by the people from the Government can be termed as direct. The direct benefit received by the respondents of Palamathi hill is presented in table 39 below.

Old Age Pension (O A P)

As shown in above table 39, 97 persons belonging to the respondent households had received old age pension. Out of them, 84 were males and 13 were females.

Farm Tools

Out of the 113 recipients of farm tools, 32 respondents had received hoe, 53 respondents had received ploughs, 25 respondents had received leveling boot, two had received iron box and one respondent had received washing machine, 61 respondents had received fertilizers at a considerable rate. Hybrid–calf was distributed to seven respondents and 29 respondents had received group house.

Horticulture

Horticulture saplings were distributed to the respondents free of cost. 45 respondents had received coconut saplings free of cost. Similarly, 45 respondents had received mango saplings, Guava saplings were distributed to 60 respondents, Pomegranate saplings were distributed to 22 respondents, 46 respondents had received lemon saplings.

The distribution of beneficiaries of various development programs among the income group shows that 281 (53.52) beneficiaries belonged to first group, 103 (19.62 per cent) belonged to second group, 65 beneficiaries (12.38 per cent) belonged to third group, 46 beneficiaries (8.76 per cent)

Table 39
Beneficiaries of Government Development Programs

S. No.	Income group (Rupees/annum)	OAP		Free Farm Tools									Horticulture				Total
		Male	*Female*	*Hoe*	*Plough*	*Leveling Boot*	*Iron Box*	*Washing Machine*	*Fertilizer*	*Calf*	*Group House*	*Coconut Saplings*	*Mango*	*Guava*	*Pomegranate*	*Lemon*	
1.	Below 12,000	63	9	13	21	12	2	1	14	2	27	17	26	33	13	28	281
2.	12,001 – 24,000	13	2	5	14	6	-	-	15	2	1	9	9	19	5	3	103
3.	24,001 – 36,000	5	1	4	12	4	-	-	13	2	1	3	7	7	4	2	65
4.	36,000 – 48,000	2	1	7	5	2	-	-	12	1	-	7	3	1	-	5	46
5.	48,001 – 64,000	1	-	3	1	1	-	-	7	-	-	9	-	-	-	8	30
	Total	84	13	32	53	25	2	1	61	7	29	45	45	60	22	46	525

Source: Primary data.

belonged to fourth group and 30 recipients (5.72 per cent) belonged to fifth group. The distribution of development programs had benefited more than 50 per cent of the lowest income group compared to the higher income groups. In other words the benefits of development programs go on decreasing with increase in income. It also confirm the second hypothesis that the development programs have helped more of the least income group than the higher income group.

Indirect Benefit

The respondents had received indirect benefits from various public goods provided by the Government like, roads, education , health, electricity, animal husbandry etc.

Child Delivery

Lack of medical facilities in Palamathi hill had forced the people to search Medicare facilities in the plain i.e, nearby town like Vellore. Table 40 provides the respondent's choice of hospitals for child delivery.

Table 40
Child Delivery

S. No.	*Income Group*	*At Home*	*Hospital in the Plain*	*Total*
1.	Below 12,000	105	84	189
2.	12,001 – 24,000	45	22	67
3.	24,001 – 36,000	38	31	69
4.	36,000 – 48,000	15	13	28
5.	48,001 – 64,000	6	7	13
	Total	209 (57..20)	157 (42.80)	366 (100.00)

Note: Figures in parenthesis are percentage to total.

Out of the 366 respondents, 209 respondents (5.7 per cent) had chosen hospital in plains for child delivery. Another revelation of the table is that there were more child deliveries at home belonging to least income group. It is the avowed policy of the Government to facilitate 100 per cent child delivery at hospitals. But this policy has not been fulfilled in the case of the people of Palamathi hills.

The group wise classification of child delivery shows that as the income increases, the child delivery at home decreases. This is applicable in all the groups as shown in the table 40.

Family Planning

Family planning has been one of the development programs implemented by the Government not only to control population but also to eradicate poverty and to improve the living standard of the people.

Out of the total of 366, 246 adopted family planning, 5 (2.03 per cent) were male, 234 (95.54 per cent) were female and 6 (2.43 per cent) were both males and females. Out of the total adaptors, 52.84 per cent belonged to least income group. It was followed by second and third group. Though sizeable number of female members had adopted family planning, still large proportion of the population remains uncovered by this program. The adaptors of family planning is also presented in Venn Diagram in Fig 7.

Fig. 7: Family Planning Adopted

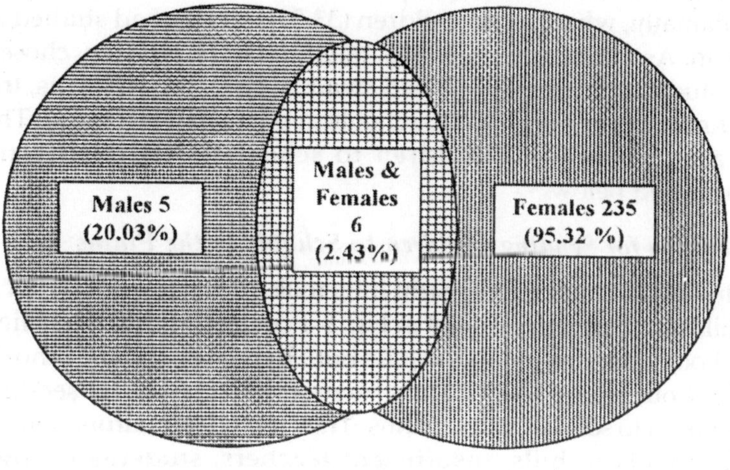

Educational Facilities

Schools are the infrastructures for learning. The infrastructures created at Palamathi hill for learning, are analyzed. Only four hamlets have primary schools run by the Government and for education above primary level, one has to go to the plains. The children's schooling is presented in table 41 below.

Table 41
Children's Schooling

S. No.	*Income Group*	*Hills*	*Plains*	*Total*
1.	Below 12,000	149	46	195
2.	12,001 – 24,000	27	61	88
3.	24,001 – 36,000	27	57	84
4.	36,000 – 48,000	19	68	87
5.	48,001 – 64,000	11	71	82
	Total	233 (43.47)	303 (56.53)	536 (100.00)

Note: Figures in parenthesis are percentage to total.

Out of the 536 children studying, 303 children (56.53 per cent) had chosen to study in the schools in plains compared to 233 children (43.47 per cent 0 who had chosen to study at Palamathi hill itself. Out of the total children belonging to first group, 149 children (76.41 per cent) had chosen to study at Palamathi, where as, 46 children (33.59per cent) had studied at plain. As the income increases, the number of children, chosen to study at Palamathi hill, had steadily declined, where as, the number of children, sent to schools at plain, had increased. The reason for sending children to schools in the plains are furnished below.

Reasons for Sending Children to Schools in the Plains

The inhabitants of Palamathi hills took efforts to educate their children. This is illustrated in Fig. 8. Primary, Middle and High School were present in the hills but Higher Secondary Schools and Colleges are absent. There were several reasons for sending children to schools in the plains. They included malfunctioning of schools in hills, insufficient teachers, students of low-standard, preference for studying in English medium and lack of high schools.

The study indicated that a majority of 61.75 per cent people had sent their children to plains as there were no high schools,

Fig. 8: Reasons for Sending Children to Schools in the Plains

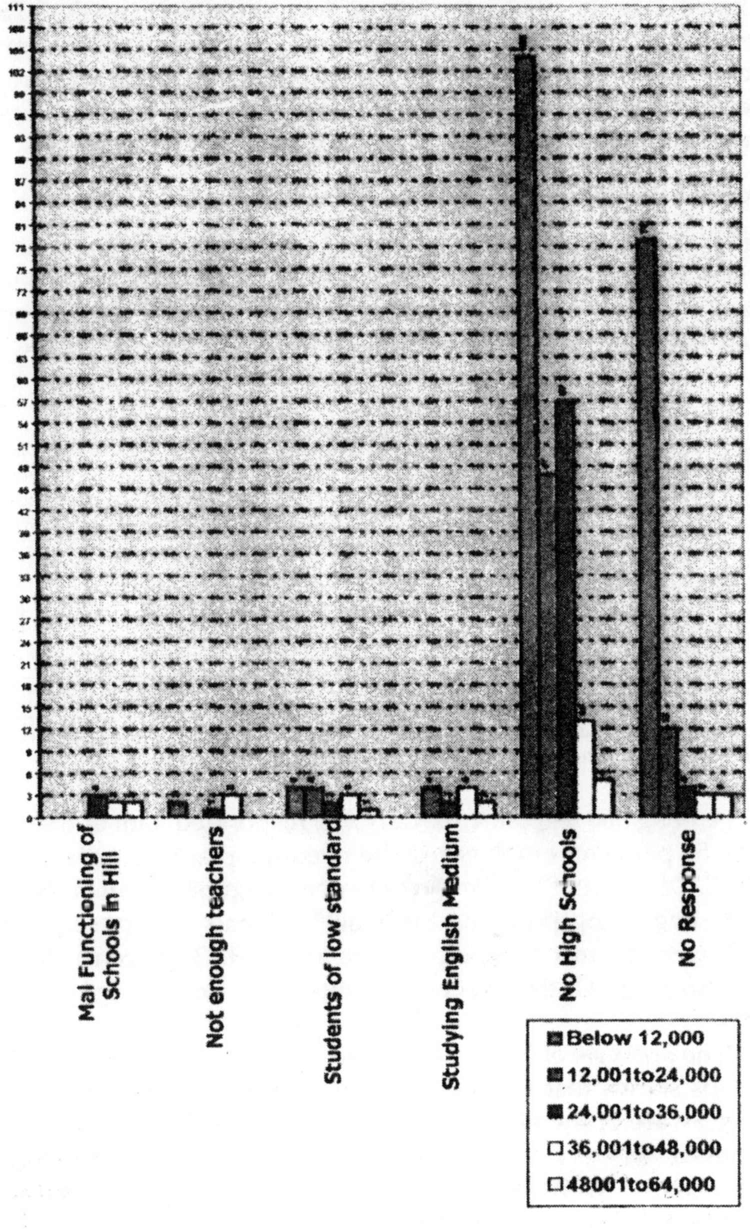

About 3.83 per cent had sent their children to plains for their schooling as the students were of low standards, while 3.28 per cent wanted their children to stay in English medium. However, 1.89 per cent felt that the schools were not functioning well and 1.64 per cent felt that there were not enough teachers and therefore they sent their children to school in the plains.

Awareness about Natural Resources

Hill people are living in the midst of resources. It is necessary to find out their level of awareness about the natural resources, ways to conserve them, and protect them from extinction. These questions were analyzed and presented in the table 42. below.

Table 42
Awareness about Natural Resources

S. No	*Income group*	*Planting trees*	*Not cutting trees*	*Poaching animals or birds*		*Grow more trees*
				Yes	*No*	
1.	Below 12,000	17	170	5	184	187
2.	12,001 – 24,000	3	63	3	64	65
3.	24,001 – 36,000	1	61	1	68	63
4.	36,000 – 48,000	2	19	1	27	25
5.	48,001 – 64,000	1	9	4	9	13
	Total	24 (6.56)	322 (87.98)	14 (3.83)	352 (96.27)	353 (100)

Note: Figures in parenthesis are percentage to total.

Among 366 respondents, only 353 responded. Out of them, 24 (6.56 per cent) emphasized the need for planting trees. But 322 (87.98 per cent) had expressed deep anguish about cutting trees. Regarding poaching birds and animals, 352 (96.27 per cent) were against poaching, where as, 14 (3.83 per cent) were for poaching. All the 353 respondents were for growing more trees.

The analysis of awareness about natural resources among groups shows that the least income group respondents were more aware of the natural resources like planting trees, not to cut trees, against poaching birds and animals and for growing more trees. On the other hand, the awareness about natural resources decreases with increase in income.

Change in Occupation

The inhabitants of Palamathi hills were migrants, travelled from far and near the hill. Is there any change in their occupation or do they continue to pursue the same occupation even now? These questions are analyzed with the details furnished in table 43.

Out of the 366 respondents, agriculture and allied activities are carried out by 91 of them, 116 (31.69 per cent) of them are coolies or landless agricultural labourers. 16 respondents were masons, four of them are tailors and three of them are Dhobis. These were traditional occupations undertaken by the respondent's parents and grandparents. The following occupations are now carried out by a small of number respondents. There were six respondents engaged in Government service, four are auto drivers, four are engaged in business, five are working as mechanics, two are working as watchmen and eight are self employed as basket weaving. 31 respondents (8.46 per cent) are engaged in non-traditional occupation.

The analysis reveals change in occupation of the inhabitants of Palamathi hill but the change has been very slow, which support the third hypothesis that change in occupation has been very slow among the inhabitants of Palamathi hill. Prevalence of illiteracy and lack of training can be attributed to this slow change in occupation. Therefore, these facilities will have to be created adequately in the hill.

Number of Persons Working in the Town

The study also aimed to assess the number of persons working in the town among the inhabitants of Palamathi hills. The number of people ranged from 1to 3 persons/family. There were a total of 45 people of Palamathi hills who worked in the town. One person each from 14 families were working in Vellore town. There was a total of 11 families that had 2 persons working in the town. In the former and latter, they were present in all the income groups unlike in 3 people from a family. That totaled 22 persons there were only 3 families that had 3 members each working in the town. It is illustrated in the following table 44.

Table 43
Change in Occupation

S. No.	Income group	Culti-vator	Cattle rearing	Govern-ment work	Coolie	Mason	Tailor	Dhobi	Car-penter	Auto	Other works: Busi-ness	Mecha-nical	Mili-tary	Watch-man	Basket weav-ing	Total
1.	Below 12,000	85	6	-	78	6	2	2	1	2	2	-	-	1	3	189
2.	12,001 – 24,000	16	-	1	36	2	1	-	2	1	-	3	-	1	4	67
3.	24,001 – 36,000	53	-	2	-	8	1	-	-	1	-	2	1	-	1	69
4.	36,000 – 48,000	20	-	2	2	-	-	1	2	-	1	-	1	-	-	28
5.	48,001 – 64,000	11	-	1	-	-	-	1	-	-	1	-	-	-	-	13
	Total	185	6	6	116	16	4	4	5	4	4	5	2	2	8	366

Note: Figures in parenthesis are per centage to total.

Table 44
Number of Persons Working in the Town

S. No.	Income group	Number of members			Total
		One	Two	Three	
1.	Below 12,000	3	2	-	5
2.	12,001 – 24,000	2	3	-	5
3.	24,001 – 36,000	2	2	2	6
4.	36,000 – 48,000	5	2	-	7
5.	48,001 – 64,000	2	2	1	5
	Total	14 x =14	11 x 3 =22	3 x 3 = 9	45

PROBLEMS AND THEIR SOLUTIONS

Problems

The respondents were asked to record the problems faced by them. The problems recorded by the respondents are scarcity of transport, absence of police station, inadequate street lights and the problems of unemployment. The table 45 gives the item wise problems recorded by the respondents.

Poor transportation network was considered as acute problem by 119 respondents (32.51 per cent). Absence of hospital also was a problem to 105 respondents (28.69 per cent). To 44 respondents (12.02 per cent), non–availability of High School was a severe problem. Water was a problem for 35 respondents (9.56 per cent). Non-availability of retail shop in the hill was felt by 24 respondents (6.56 per cent). Seven respondents felt the need for a police station. Absence of adequate street light was a problem to 8 respondents (2.19 per cent). 24 respondents (6.56 per cent) recorded unemployment as a severe problem.

Suggestions

The following suggestions were made by the respondents as a remedy for the above problems. The suggestions are illustrated in Fig. 9. Establishment of factories at Palamathi hills were suggested by 103 respondents (28.14 per cent), 93 respondents recommended to make the forest development programs effective. Making Palamathi a hill resort, was suggested by 77

Table 45
Problems

S. No.	Income group	*Scarcity of transport*	*Absence of hospital*	*Non-availability of schools*	*Water problem*	*Absence of retail shop*	*Absence of police station*	*Absence of proper light*	*Unemploy-ment problem*	*Total*
1.	Below 12,000	52	62	23	17	13	5	3	14	189
2.	12,001 – 24,000	29	15	10	4	3	-	1	5	67
3.	24,001 – 36,000	24	17	5	9	5	2	2	5	69
4.	36,000 – 48,000	6	9	4	5	3	-	1	-	28
5.	48,001 – 64,000	8	2	2	-	-	-	1	-	13
	Total	119	105	44	35	24	7	8	24	366

Note: Figures in parenthesis are percentage to total.

respondents (8.47 per cent). 37 respondents (10.11 per cent) had made the recommendation to start high school and to provide educational facilities. 25 respondents (6.83 per cent) suggested to increase the frequency of transport in the hilŀ.

These recommendations, if fulfilled, will help solve the problems of the inhabitants. Therefore, it is high time to adopt suitable action plan by the government, private and voluntary organizations, to help the inhabitants realize their dreams by implementing the programs.

NOTES

1. J.E. Park and K. Park, Op cit, p. 273.
2. Ajit B. Jain (2002), "Limited investment but consistent growth". The Hindu survey of Indian Agriculture, pp. 147–149
3. Sivanappan R.K. (2002), "Expansion of storage capacity critical" The Hindu Survey of Indian Agriculture, Pg. 183-186.
4. Kadirvel R. (2002), "Limited investment but consistent growth" The Hindu Survey of Indian Agriculture, Pg. 147-149.
5. Grewal P.S., op cit, p. 169.

6

SUMMARY, CONCLUSION AND POLICY IMPLICATIONS

SUMMARY

Problem Focus

One third of the earth surface is covered by land and two-third by water. It can be further classified into mountain areas, plain and coastal area. 10 per cent of the world's population depends directly or indirectly on mountains. Thus the importance of mountains in the life of people can not be undermined. The main occupation of the people in the mountain areas is agriculture. Though the mountain dwellers look like people in the plain, their problems and challenges are entirely different from the plains. Transportation to hill is a hazardous task. All people residing in the mountainous regions are not treated as 'tribes' as many of them live below the required height. Thus, they forfeit the privileges accorded to the tribal population. Not much studies have been made on the socio-economic condition of the people in the mountain areas. Hence the present study, to fill the gap, has been under taken.

The Palamathi hill has been purposely chosen for the present study because 95 per cent of the inhabitants are migrants. It is possible to find out the change in their life style after their arrival to the hill. Since the hill is closer to Vellore town, the urban influence on the life of the inhabitants can also be noticed. The issues involved in the present analysis are: what is the present socio-economic condition of the inhabitants of Palamathi hill? what are the development programs implemented in the village? And how far have the people derived benefit from these programs?

The objectives adopted for the present study are: to trace the origin and settlement details of the inhabitants of the Palamathi hills, to examine the socio-economic conditions of the inhabitants of Palamathi hills, to analyze the level of poverty prevailing among the people of Palamathi hills, and to identify and describe the role played by the development programs undertaken in the Palamathi hills.

The following hypothesis were adopted for analysis, they are: (1) The migrants of Palamathi hills have traveled from far and near to the hill. (2) The development programs have benefited more of the least income group in the hill than the higher income group. (3) There has been a slow change in the occupation of the inhabitants of Palamathi hills.

The Approach

Review of Concepts and Past Studies

The following concepts and past studies were reviewed for the purpose of the present study:

- Settlement
- Migration
- Hill Economics
- Socio-Economic Condition
- Consumption
- Marketed Surplus
- Income
- Expenditure
- Saving
- Investment
- Borrowing
- Poverty

- Employment
- Development

Methodology

In the explorative study, both secondary and primary data were found to be useful. The secondary data were collected from published sources like Vellore District Gazetteers, Tamilnadu Government Publications, District collector's office, Vellore, Tamilnadu and Economic Appraisal, Rural Development, Bulletins, Government of India publications relating to five year plants and Gramodya etc.

The primary data were collected from all the households of Palamathi hills, distributed among five hamlets, by adopting Census method. Pre-tested interview schedule was used to collect the required details from the respondents. The Panchayat President, Mr. N.K. Ragavan, who has been the president for more than 40 years, was interview personally in order to collect more details about the change occurred in the hill. The State Government Officials at the village, taluk and district level were interview with a view to gather more information about the hill.

Both descriptive and quantitative tools were applied for the analysis of data. Descriptive method are: simple averages, percentages, graphs and diagrams.

The following quantitative tools were used for analysis:

- Correlation Method
- Correlation Matrix
- Regression Analysis
- Elasticity of Market Surplus
- Trend in the Migration of Respondents
- t- test

The Dimensions

The special features of Palamathi hill have been enlightened by its location, elevation, administrative set up, topography, geology, climate, precipitation, drainage, irrigation, soil, ground water, land use pattern, cropping pattern, population, birth and death rate, literacy, occupation, socio-economic change, housing, family structure, method of cultivation, irrigation, fertilizers, mode of transport, fuel, entertainment, infrastructure, roads, transport, water supply, electricity, communication systems, schools, development activities, forest development schools, places of worship, deities and festivals, tourism, tourist spots etc.

THE RESULTS

The primary data, collected by adopting census method from all the households of Palamathi hills, were analyzed under seven sections.

Classification of Respondents

The households were classified into five groups according to their annual income.

Classification and Settlement

Almost all the inhabitants of Palamathi hills were migrants. They migrated from nearly 40 places located in Vellore district of Tamilnadu, Andhra Pradesh and Karnataka Who migrated to Palamathi first? The answers to this question was not uniform. In some cases, grandparents had migrated while in some, parents has migrated and in some others, the present generation, irrespective of the sex had migrated. Though the first exodus had begun as early as 1886, migration to Palamathi had continued at reduced rate till 2000. The calculated trend line, had shown a fall in migration to Palamathi since 1950. Among the various reasons for migrations to Palamathi hill, search for land and job were considered to be significant factors. The migrants had traveled between one to 25 kilometers to reach Palamathi hills.

The nature of job done by these migrants, showed that most of them were engaged in agriculture or worked as agriculture coolies. The life expectancy of the migrants revealed that the average life expectancy of females (69.6 years) was higher than the males (66.88 years).

Social Status

The social status of the inhabitants of Palamathi hills was analyzed under eight sub headings: it exhibited high incidence of illiteracy among the respondents. But most of the illiterates belonged to lowest income group. The level of education indicate the growing awareness among the respondents about the need for education. The relationship between income and education was analyzed with t-test. The result of the t-analysis shows that the illiterates and literates had similar means of income.

The gender wise classification of respondents revealed that there were 323 male headed families as against 43 female headed families.

The age indicates that the respondents, both male and female belonged to the ageing group.

The distribution of respondents among various castes had disclosed that there were 45 respondents belonging to scheduled caste, 220 respondents belonging to most backward class and 101 respondents belonged to backward class.

The average size of families of the respondents was calculated as 5.93. But the average size of families varied with size of income. It warrants immediate attention on the family education program carried on at Palamathi hills.

Regarding the type of families, nuclear families are expanding, whereas the joint families and extended families are vanishing.

R.C.C. roof houses were popular among the inhabitants of Palamathi hill, as many of them (37.15 per cent) had constructed houses with R.C.C. roof. The low income group had predominantly Kutcha, thatched and tiled houses.

Economic Status

The economic status of the respondents in Palamathi hill was analyzed under assets, irrigation, livestock ownership of vehicles, nature of employment, cropping pattern, total value of produce sold, average value of crops sold, production of paddy, marketed surplus of paddy, marketing of produce, income, annual expenditure, comparison of annual income and expenditure, saving, borrowing and investment.

Though land is the major sources of assets of the majority of the respondents, 133 respondents were landless. Even among those who owned land, the size of land had ranged between one to four acres. On the basis of size of land, the respondents, who owned land, could be termed as marginal and small land owners. Among the owners of land, the nature of land owned by them either wet, dry, garden or both. Only 233 respondents had used irrigation facilities, mostly from open wells.

The livestock formed an important source of assets to the respondents. the value of livestock, owned by them, had ranged between Rs. 5,000 to 10,000.

Among the respondents, 143 of them owned vehicles. Bicycles were used by most of the respondents. Other vehicles used by the respondents, were motorized two wheelers such as scooter and mopeds and also four wheelers viz., lorry, auto, tractor and car.

The nature of employment displayed different types of labour like family labour and public service. The cropping pattern discloses area under each crop. The respondents had evinced interest in multi crop rather than mono-crops.

Both the total value of crops sold and average value of crops sold by the respondents were calculated. Though the total value of the crop was highest among the least income group, it was noticed that the average value of crop sold was highest among upper income group.

The total and average production of paddy of the respondents were estimated The average production of paddy had increased with the increase in the size of income.

The marketed surplus of paddy was higher among the lower income group than with the high income group. The percentage of marketed surplus to total production had demonstrated increase in the percentage of marketed surplus with increase in size of income. The correlation matrix of variables had established close relationship between net area, out put, consumption and expenditure. The regression analysis on marketed surplus had indicated that the net area played a predominant role in predicting the marketed surplus.

Most of the agriculture produces, produced by the respondents, were sold through the Vellore market. Microscopic quantity of produce was sold at the village and at the Salem market.

Among the various sources of income, wages formed a major share of gross income. It was followed by income from crop, milk, other sources and animals.

Among the various items of expenditure, expenditure on food stands first, followed by expenditure on beverages, entertainment, medicine, clothes, festivals, transport, and electricity.

Comparison of annual income and expenditure had indicated surplus income over expenditure in all the groups. A very high degree of correlation between annual income and expenditure was brought out by the correlation analysis.

Out of the 366 respondents, only 26 were able to save. They saved between Rs. 5,000 to Rs. 25,000.Money lenders formed the major source of lending. The other sources were banks, cooperatives, traders and relatives. The amount borrowed was utilized for both productive and unproductive purposes.

About 50 respondents had made investments, ranging between Rs. 25,000 to Rs. 2,00,000. The items of investment varies from house construction to livestock, digging wells and deepening wells.

Poverty at Palamathi Hills

Poverty prevailing among the households at Palamathi hills was studied under the poverty of income, poverty of assets, caste wise poverty, child labour, and basic amenities.

As per the classification of households according to annual income, 189 households were included in the first group, whose annual income was less than Rs. 12,000. Those households were deemed to be under poverty. As against this, there were only 140 households that were included in the BPL (Below the Poverty Line) list.

Majority of the respondents, belonged to the first group, were landless labourers working as coolies. Except wages, they had no other sources of income.

Out of the 189 respondents, 17 respondents belonged to the Scheduled Caste and 140 respondents belonged to weaker section. The weaker sections were prevailing in all committees and in all hamlets.

Child labourers were found to be in 43 families at Palamathi hills in the age group of 5 to 14years in both sexes. Highest incidence of child labourers was present in the least income group compared to the second and third group. The other higher income groups had no child labourers.

Regarding distribution of drinking water , tap was available only to 223 households. 40 per cent of the households could not avail themselves of electric connection so far. 359 households were accessible to dry latrines. It shows the poor levels of living of the people in the study area.

Development Programs

Various development programs were implemented in order to develop the Palamathi hills. These programs could be classified as general programs and specific programs. They were further classified as direct and indirect programs. Out of 366 households, 97 households had received old age pension (OAP), 113 households had received farm tools, and 218 households had received free horticulture saplings. It was observed that the development programs had brought more benefit to least income group than to the higher income groups.

Lack of medical facilities at the hill had forced the people to go to the hospitals in plain for child delivery. Though, family planning programs were undertaken in the hill, only 234 persons had adopted family planning, which includes both males and females. Nearly fifty per cent of the persons belonging to least income group had adopted family planning.

The educational facilities available at the hill were not attractive to the children. Therefore, nearly 303 children, out of 536 children, had chosen to study in the schools at the plains by traveling 8 to 10 kilometers. Various reasons attributed for going to schools at the plains were: malfunctioning of schools, not enough teachers, low standard, preference for English medium, lack of High school etc.

The survey revealed high degree of awareness among the inhabitants about natural resources and their conservation. They expressed their awareness through planting trees and growing more trees, as against cutting trees and poaching animals or birds.

As a result of various development programs, undertaken at the hills, change in occupation of the inhabitants was discernible but it was very slow. Reverse migration could also be observed. Out of the working population, 45 persons were working in the nearby towns in various capacities.

Problems and Solutions

Various problems, reported by the respondents were: scarcity of transport, absence of hospital, non-availability of high school, water problem, absence of retail shops, absence of police station, absence of proper street light and unemployment.

Various suggestions, given by the respondents, to solve the problems include: establishment of factories, effective development programs to make Palamathi a hill resort, removing water scarcity, improving education facilities and to increasing frequency of transport. Effective implementation of these suggestions would improve the living condition of the inhabitants of the hill.

CONCLUSION

The following conclusions could be drawn from the above summary of findings.

1. The inhabitants, migrated from various places in plains, continue to live at the hill. It shows their love of nature in spite of various hardships.
2. The higher income group enjoys better social status in terms of literacy and housing. The low income group suffers from various social disabilities like illiteracy and poor housing.
3. The low economic condition of the poor households could be attributed to lack of assets, low wages, unemployment and debt. But the high income group had enjoyed better

economic condition due to ownership of land, livestock and vehicles.

4. In cropping pattern, the respondents had grown multi-crops in different types of land. Production of paddy had increased with the size of farms. Therefore, the average marketed surplus generated in the farms was more in large farms than in small farms.
5. The majority of inhabitants had marketed their produce through Vellore market in spite of transport problems.
6. Wages formed major component of gross income of the households. Therefore the enhancement of wage rate would push up the economic status of the people in the hill.
7. All the groups had generated surplus income over expenditure. This surplus income could be converted into assets if proper facilities are created to save through institutions and incentives.
8. More than 50 per cent of the respondents were debtors. Majority of them had borrowed from money lenders. It is, therefore, necessary to strengthen the institutions in the area.
9. Only a small group of respondents had made attempts to invest. It shows inter alia that proper climate for investment has not been created.
10. Majority of low income group of people found to be living in poverty. Therefore, it is necessary to strengthen the asset base of the households, generate employment (self/paid) and to improve their skills through literacy and training.
11. The raison d'etre of the development programs is to raise the standard of living of the people. But the development programs had touched only a small group of people. The development programs, undertaken at the Palamathi hills, had brought more benefits to least income group than to high income group. It brings solace. But it should be further strengthened, so that, every body receives benefits from the programs. The impact of the development programs on the inhabitants has not been effective because the change in occupation has been very slow.

12. The high degree of awareness about the resources at the hill is a positive aspect to be preserved and promoted. It ipso facto reveals that the inhabitants have identified themselves with nature.

POLICY IMPLICATIONS

The following suggestions are made for policy and the adoption of these suggestions would ameliorate the socio-economic condition of the inhabitants of the Palamathi hills.

1. Most of the problems of the inhabitants center around employment, low wages, lack of assets and infrastructural facilities. Therefore, the inhabitant's demand for factories in the hill can be met by developing smokeless industry, and tourism, which has plenty of job opportunities.
2. Most of the landless labourers depend on their wage for their survival . By implementing the Minimum Wages Act for agricultural labourers strictly, it would improve their living condition.
3. As most of the people in the hill depend on agriculture, distribution of forest land to the landless people would generate employment and income to them.
4. Infrastructural facilities like roads, educational facilities, medical facilities, electric connection, water connection can be created in the hill, which will remove the concern of many inhabitants.
5. The people of the hill depend on agriculture for their livelihood, therefore, the production condition in the hill farm should be improved by means of creating irrigation facilities, supply of inputs at low price, providing timely information and credit at concessional rate.
6. Recognition of the hill as special and distinct from low land would facilitate resource flows to and from the hill, which will lead to increased income to hill communities and fair distribution of earnings from natural resources and services.
7. The problem of wants of the inhabitants of the Palamathi hills could be mitigated by providing potable water supply,

hospital, transport, schools and retail shops. Figure 13 explains the problems and its mitigation.

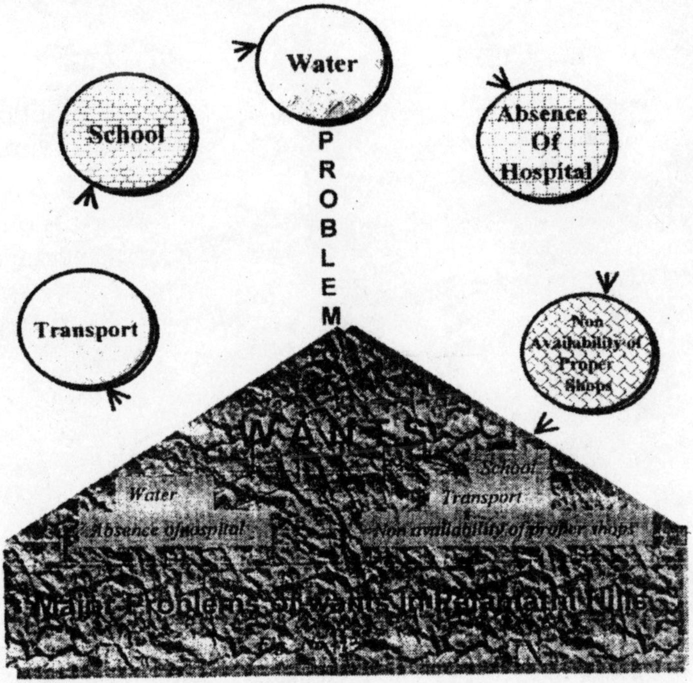

BIBLIOGRAPHY

BOOKS

Agrlvala. S.N. and Singha. V.P. (1901), "Indian Population Problems", Tata MC.Graw -Hill, New Delhi, p. 217.

Anon (1936), "Social Forestry Schemes", Council for Advancement of peoples Action and Rural Technology. Bengal off set works, New Delhi, p. 1.

Anon Statistical Outline of India (2000-2001), Tata services Limited, Department of Economics and Statistics. Bombay house Mumbai-400001, p. 32.

Arockiasamy (1981) ,"Economic Analysis", Shanthi Publishing House, Tirunelveli, p. 183.

Bhaskar G. (1994), "Trends in Rural Poverty", RBSA Publication, Jaipur, pp. 1-7.

Boyce Ronald R. (1974), "The Basis of Economic Geography", Holt Rinehart and Winston Publishers, U.S.A, p. 56.

Carold Rakodi (2002), "A livelihood Approach-Conceptual Issues and Definition" in the book "Urban Livelihoods-A People Centred Approach to reducing Poverty", Carold Rakodi and Tony Lioyd-Jones U.S.A, p. 328.

Carr-Harris J. (Ed) (1995), "Mountains and People-A peoples perspective from the Indian Himalayas". Sri Bhuvaneswari Mahila Ashram. Paper presented at the NGO consultation, Sustainable Development, Lima, Peru, p. 6.

Cooling Wood L. (1983), "21st Century Universal Encyclopedia", Vol . 26, Regency Publishing, Sydney, p. 49.

Desai A.R. (1969), "Fundamentals of Rural Economics", Himalaya Publishing House Bombay, p. 120.

Dewett, K.K. and Sundram K.P.M. *et al*, (2000), "Indian Economics", S. Chand & Company, New Delhi, 2000, p. 455.

District Census Book, Vellore, (1991).

Dubey (1992), "Process of Socio-Economic Development", Rawat Publications, Jaipur, p. 155.

Dulhashi. P.R. (1997), "Potentialities and Limitations of Co-operations for Integrated Rural Development, Co-operative News Digest", Vol. XXVIII, (6), p. 68.

Ghodake.N.B. (1986), "Encyclopedic Dictionary of Economics," Volume 5, Mital Publications, New Delhi, pp. 640, 641.

Gohcheng and Morgan Gillian C. (1988), "Human and Economic Geography", Oxford University Press, Oxford, p. 33.

Grewal (1985), " Rural Economics", Kalyani Publishers, New Delhi, p. 82.

"Harijan" (1936), Selection from Gandhi", p. 71.

Harish Chandra Singh (1989),"Rural Environment Development and Planning", Chugh Publications, Allahabad, p. 122.

James M. Rubenstein, *et al*, (1990),"The Cultural Landscape-An Introduction to Human geography", Prentice Hall of India, New Delhi, pp. 342, 343, 344.

John Black (1997), "A Dictionary of Economics", Oxford University Press, New York, p. 229.

Khanna K.K.and Gupta V.K. (1994), "Economic and Commercial Geography", Sultan Chand & and Sons, New Delhi, p. 10.1.

Kindle Berger Charles P. and Bruce Herrick (1958), "Economic Development", Mc Graw Hill, Chicago Inc, p. 2.

Kindle Berger Charles P.(1965) , "Economic Development", Mc. Graw Hill, New York, p. 3.

Kingsly Davis (1995), "Human Society", Surjeet Publications", Delhi, p. 590.

Kurnati Lingaiah (1991), "Dictionary of Economics", Link Publications, Bharatpur, p. 21.

Mamoria. C.B. (1981), "Social Problems and Social Disorganization in India", Kitab Mahal, Allahabad, pp. 270, 271.

Mahajan V.S. (1990), "Agriculture and Rural Economy in India", Deep & Publications, New Delhi, p. 350.

Meier & Baldwin (1976), "Economic Development–Theory, History, Policy", Asia Publishing House, New Delhi, p. 2.

Mosby Medical Encyclopedia (1992), Published in New York City, p. 360.

Ngugi. D.N., P.K. Karau, and W. Nguyo (1992), "East African Agriculture", Macmillan, London, p. 216.

Nortan Peter B. and Joseph J. (1994) "The New Encyclopaedia Britannica" , Inc-Volume 9, Esposito President, Publishing Group, Chicago, p. 652.

Oomen Priyan C. (1989), "Global's Tourism Directory of India "Global Communication, Trivandurm, p. 1.

Padmanabhan K. (1997) "Economic Transition with a Human Face", I.I. P.A, Tirupattur Local Branch, pp. 1-12.

Park J.E. and K. Park (1991), "Park's Text book of preventive and Social Medicine", Banarsidas Bharat Publishers, Jebalpur, p.12.

Pushpa Indurkar (1992), "Forestry, Environment and Economic Development", Ashish Publishing Houses New Delhi, p. 3.

Rai B.C. (1988), "Education and Society-A Study of Sociological foundation of Education" Prakashan Kendra, Luknow, pp. 3,5.

Raj. K.N. (1977) , "Village India and its Political Economy", University of Madras, pp.1-12.

Rajesh R. and Kombairraju S. (1999), "Impact of Technological change on Women Employment in Dry Land Agriculture", Indian Journal of Agricultural Economics, Vol. 54, (2) pp. 302, 303.

Rowntree B.S. (1902), "Poverty", A Study of Turn life Macmillan, London, p. XVII.

Ruddar Datt and Sundharam K.P.M. (2001), "Indian Economy", S. Chand & Company, New Delhi, p. 469.

Sadhu and Singh (1968), "Fundamentals of Agricultural Economics", Himalaya Publishing House, Bombay, p. 252.

Sadhukhan S.K. (1982), "Economic Geography", An Appraisal of Resources," S. Chand & Company, New Delhi, p. 11.

Saxena D.P. (1994), "Rural Towns and Socio-Economic Development of Villages", with Special Reference to Eastern U.P. Mittal Publications, New Delhi, pp. 27-29.

Spencer Hatch D. (1936), "Up from Poverty in Rural India", Oxford University Press, Madras, pp. 184-186.

Samuelson Paul A. and William D. Nordhaus (1995), "Economics", Mc.Graw-Hill, Inc, New York, p. 362.

"The World Book of Encyclopedia" (1959), Chicago, Field Enterprises Educational Corporation, Merchandise Martplaya, Volume 8, p. 3421.

Umaleli (1975), "Design of Rural Development, Lessons from Africa", Baltimore, John Hopkins Press, p. 20.

Vaish (2002) "Macro Economic Theory", Vikas Publishing House, New Delhi, pp. 155,156.

Varma S.C. (1984), "Millions in Poverty Grip", Kunji Publishing House, New Delhi, p. 15.

Wilbur G.L. (ed.) (1973), "Poverty-A New Perspective", The University Press of Kentucky, Lexington, p. 6.

Yadava. K.N.S. (1992), "Rural Urban Commutation and Rural Development", Shipra Publications, New Delhi, pp. 141-153.

JOURNALS

Ajit B. Jain (2002), "Improper Technologies Could Jeopardize further". The Hindu Survey of Indian Agriculture, pp.183-186.

Anon, (1981), "Social Science Research and the Problem of Poverty", ICSSR, First National Conference on Social Sciences, New Delhi, Volume: (1, 2 & 3), p. 42.

Anon (1985), "Demographic Perspective In Poverty", IASSI, Vol. 4, p. 5.

Anoop Singh Dhukia and Sharma R.K., "Constraints in Socio-Economic Development of Village," Kurukshetra, Vol. 46, (9), 1998, pp. 28-30.

Balbir Kumar and Karam Singh (1992), "Socio-Economic Problems of Tribal Gujjars in Punjab", IASSI Quarterly, Vol. II, (2), pp. 157-161.

Baldev Singh (1988), "Science, Technology and Eradication of rural poverty", IASSI Quarterly Bulletin, Vol.72(23), pp. 83-86.

Bharwaj S.P. and Gupta H.C. (1991), "An Optimum Utilization of Land Resources", Indian Journal of Agricultural Economics, Vol. 46, (3) pp. 384, 385.

Dhanasekharan K. (1991), "Socio-Economic Measures of Quality of Rural Life", An Alternative Approach for Measures in Rural Poverty", Indian Journal of Agricultural Economics , Vol. XLVI, (1), pp. 34-43.

Ganesh. A.(1985), "Micro Level Plan for Rural Development", Kurukshetra, Vol. 33 (5), pp. 30,31.

Jairath M.S. and Shanti Sarup (1991), "Regional Variation in Agricultural Development, Agricultural situation in India, New Delhi, pp. 15-17.

Kanta Prasad (1989), "Socio-Economic Requirements or Appropriate Technologies for Eradication of Rural Poverty ", IASSI, Quarterly Journal, Vol. 8 (I) pp. 65-71.

Kadirvel R. (2002), "Limited Investment but Consistent Growth". The Hindu Survey of Indian Agriculture, pp.147-149.

Kas G.C. (1989), "Conceptual Considerations on Poverty", Journal of Rural Development, Vol. 8 (3), pp. 263-268.

Kingsly Davis (1947), "Future Migration in to Latin America", Milk Bank Memorial Fund Quarterly, Vol. 25, pp. 44, 62.

Narayana K.V., Ram Reddy M. (1989), "Development Schemes for Rural Poor", Kurukshetra, Vol. 37(7), pp. 43-45.

Narayana Reddy G. (1989), "Socio-Psychological Determinants of Poverty", Journal of Rural Development", Vol. 8 (4), p. 371-379.

Nagabushana Rao E. (1989), "Planning Units for Rural Development- A Study", Kurukshetra, Vol . XXXVII (6), pp. 49,50.

Obsol, R.C., Chandel B.S., *et al.* (1993),"Socio-Economic Status and Constraints of Tribal Economy", Kinnaura of Himachal Pradesh, IASS Quarterly ,Vol. 122, (5), pp. 173-175.

Pant K.P. and Pandey V.K. (1999), "Minimizing Environmental Problems in Hill Agriculture of Nepal through Multi Objective Farm Planning", Indian Journal of Agricultural Economics, Vol. 54, (4), pp. 79-83.

Paramjit Kaurchawhan (1998), "Migration of Women Labour and their Problems", Southern Economist, Vol. 37, (15) p. 9.

Ramesh Chand and Tewari S.C. (1991), "Factors Affecting Land–Market Transactions and its Impact on Size Distribution of Holdings in Hill Region", Indian Journal of Agricultural Economics, Vol. XLVI, (3), p. 365.

Sadanandam A. and Bhakar G. (1989), "Concept of Rural Poverty", Kurukshetra ,Vol. 37 (12), pp. 39-43.

Sharma A.K. (1989), "What the Poor think about Their Poverty? A Socio-Psychological Study", the Indian Journal of Social Work, Vol. 50 (2), pp. 171-181.

Sharma.M.L., Jagadish Kumar, *et al.* (1993), "Cost and Return Analysis of Black Gram (*Phaseolus mungo*) in Uttar Pradesh hills", Indian Journal of Agricultural Economics, Vol. XLVIII, (2), pp. 430,431.

Saraswat S.P. and Dahiya Prem S. (1998), "Pattern and Economics of Energy Use in Hill Agriculture A Case of Himachal Pradesh". Indian Journal of Agriculture Economics, Vol. 53, (3), pp. 310.

Sujit Sikidan (1988), "Problems of Institutional Finance in Hill Areas", Kurukshetra, Vol. 37(3), pp. 26-29.

Sivanappan, R.K. (2002), "Expansion of Storage Capacity, Critical". The Hindu Survey of Indian Agriculture, pp. 179-181.

Swarn Lata Arya & Mittal S.P. (1992), "Managing Hill Resources thro' Community Participation", Kurukshetra ,Vol. XL, (4), pp. 15-18.

Tripathi R.S. (1996), "Pattern of Investment of Fixed Assets and Capital Formation in Different Subsistence Hill Farming Systems of Uttar Pradesh", Indian Journal of Agricultural Economics, Vol. 51, (4), pp. 626, 627.

Tripathi R.S. (1998), "Level and Pattern of Energy Use in the Hill Farming System of Uttrakhand", Indian Journal of Agricultural Economics", Vol. 53, (3), pp. 20, 281.

Thamarajakshi R. (1939), "Agricultural Growth, Rural Development and Employment Generation", Economic and Political Weekly, Vol. XXVI, (12), pp. A.5 A.8.

Udaya Bhaskara Reddy (1986), "Socio-Economic Conditions of Rural Poor, Kurukshetra, Vol. XXIV, (6), pp. 18-20.

Vasanthi K. (2000), "Poverty a Social Insecurity", Kurukshetra, Vol. 48, (8), pp. 46-48.

ANNEXURE

Socio-economic Conditions of the Inhabitants of Palamathi Hills In Tamilnadu.

INTERVIEW SCHEDULE

RESEARCHER: CODE No:

GUIDE : Date :

Name Age Sex- M/F

Door No: Village name :

Social Status

Education

Caste

Occupation

Primary Occupation-head of the Family (HOF)

Wife-________________

Sons 1.________________ 2.________________

3.________________ 4.________________

Daughters 1.________________ 2.________________

3.________________ 4.________________

Father of HOF ________________

Mother of HOF ________________

Secondary occupation–head of the family (HOF)

Wife ________________

Sons 1.________________ 2.________________

3.________________ 4.________________

Daughters 1.________________ 2.________________

3.________________ 4.________________

Father of HOF ________________

Mother of HOF ________________

Origin and settlement

Place of birth

Is it the same place or different place?

If it is different place, give details of the place

Name of the place

Name of the District

Name of the State

Distance of the place of Migration

Who Migrated?

Self	Y/N, Year ________
Father	Y/N, Year ________
Mother	Y/N, Year ________
Grand father/Grand mother	Y/N, Year ________

Reasons for Migration

Lack of land

Lack of employment

Social problem–Caste discrimination

Religious problem–religious compulsion

Any other (Specify)

Occupation of Grand Parents

Age of Grand Father at the time of death

Age of Grand Mother at the time of death

Family Status

Total Number of Members

Type of family

Joint family

Extended family

Nuclear family

Relationship in the family

S. No.	*Name*	*Relationship to the head*	*Education status*	*Marital*	*Occupation*	*Income/ month (Rupees)*
1.						
2.						
3.						
4.						

Child Labour: Yes/No If yes, specify the number

Assets:

House–Own/Rented/Allotted

If own nature of the house–Kutcha/Thatched/Tiled/RCC roof

If rented monthly rent

Land

wet (acres) ______________

Dry (acres) ______________

Garden (acres) ______________

Total (acres) ______________

Irrigation

open well/bore well

electric pump/oil pump

Cropping Pattern

S. No.	*Name of the crop*	*Area (acres)*	*Production (quintals)*	*Consumption (quintals)*	*Sold (quintals)*	*Place sold*	*Price received (Rs)*
1.							
2.							
3.							
4.							

*Hills /Plains

Livestock

S. No.	*Livestock*	*Number*	*Value*
1.			
2.			
3.			
4.			

Milk yielding Animals:

S. No.	*Type of animal*	*Daily yield (in litres)*	*Value of milk*
1.			
2.			
3.			
4.			

Vehicle owned

S. No.	*Type of vehicle*	*Value (rupees)*
1.	Country cart	
2.	Bicycle	
3.	Tractor	
4.	Scooter	
5.	Car (4 Wheeler)	

Income

Annual income from

	Amount (Rs.)
Sale of crops	____________
Sale of animals	____________
Sale of milk	____________
Wage received	____________
Other Sources	____________
Total	____________

Employment

S. No.	*Type of labour*	*Male*	*Female*	*Children*
1.	Family labour			
2.	Paid labour			
3.	Attached labour			

Expenditure

Food	*Daily*	*Rupees*

Main items of food–

- Rice, wheat
- Ragi, cumbu, cholam
- Small millets
- Vegetables
- Fruits
- Eggs
- Meat
- Fish

Beverages–alcohol

- F.M.I.L.
- Tea
- Coffee

Entertainments

Clothing

Others–medicines

- Electricity
- Transport
- Festival (annual)

Savings

S. No.	*Source of savings*	*Amount saved (Rs.)*
1	Bank	
2	Co-operative society	
3	Private	
4	Relatives	

Investment

S. No	Quantum of investments	Tick a ✓
1	< 25,000	☐
2	25,001 to 50,000	☐
3	50,001 to 1,00,000	☐
4	1,00,000 to 2,00,000	☐

Borrowings

S. No.	Source of borrowing	Amount borrowed	Purpose
1	Bank		
2	Co-operative society		
3	Traders		
4	Relatives		
5	Money lenders		

Frequency of travel to Vellore/other places

S. No.	Mode	Place to	Purpose
1			
2			
3			
4			

Basic Amenities at home

Drinking water-tap/bore/open well

Electricity connection

Sanitation-wet/dry

Disposal of Waste-pit/open place

Consumer items used

(a) Fan (b) TV (c) Radio

(d) Phone connection (e) Mixie (f) Grinder

(g) Fridge (h) Washing machine

(i) Gas/Gobar gas (j) Furniture

Health Affected by any other Disease

S. No.	*Disease*	*Man*	*Women*	*Children*
1	Polio			
2	Blindness			
3	Fever			
4	Headache			
5	Stomachache			
6	Back pain			
7	Cancer			
8	AIDS			
9	Any other			

PHC Doctors ———— Nurses ———— Beds ————

Child delivery-at home/in the hill/in hospital/in the plain

Family planning adopted -Yes /No

If yes, male ———— female ———— both ————

School facility

Children sent to schools in the hills

Children sent to schools in the plains

If Children are sent to the plains give reasons

Schools in hills not functioning properly

Adequate teachers are not available

Teachers are not regular

Students are not looked after properly

Standard of students is poor

Participation in the Social Activity

Voting during the election

Panchayat Yes/No

Assembly Yes/No

Parliament Yes/No

If no, give reason——————————————————

Membership in

A Panchayat Yes/No

Co-op Society Yes /No

Any other body Yes/No

Preservation of Natural Resources

How do you help in the preservation of natural resources?

Planting trees in the farm (how many?)——————————

Not grazing the cattle in the farm

Cutting forest trees (number)

Your opinion about green coverage-Good/Bad

Do you poach wild animals or birds?

How do you help the Government to grow more trees?

Poverty Indices

Your BPL number

Number of persons who received OAP-Males————— Females—————

Any other benefit got from the government?specify —————

Social Customs

Inter caste marriage Yes/No

Widow remarriage Yes/No

Dowry paid Yes/No

Education to girls Yes/No

Your Problems in the Hills

1 ——————————— 2 ———————————

3 ——————————— 4 ———————————

5 ——————————— 6 ———————————

Number of people working in the town specify

Suggestion to solve these problems